Hands-On Python and CNT

A Practical Guide to Deep Learning and AI Development

Sarful Hassan

Preface

Artificial Intelligence (AI) and Deep Learning are transforming industries worldwide, and mastering these technologies is crucial for developers, researchers, and data scientists. **Hands-On Python and CNTK** is a practical guide designed to help you understand and implement AI models using **Microsoft's Cognitive Toolkit (CNTK)**. Whether you're a beginner or an experienced professional, this book provides a **hands-on approach to building neural networks, training deep learning models, and optimizing performance using CNTK**.

With a focus on **practical applications**, this book walks you through **real-world examples, code implementations, and best practices** for deep learning with Python and CNTK. By the end of this book, you will have a strong foundation in CNTK and be able to build AI models for tasks such as **computer vision, natural language processing (NLP), time series forecasting, and reinforcement learning**.

Who This Book Is For

This book is intended for:

- **Machine learning engineers** looking to integrate CNTK into their workflows.

- **Data scientists and AI researchers** interested in exploring deep learning techniques.

- **Python developers** who want to expand their skills into AI and deep learning.

- **Students and academics** studying artificial intelligence and neural networks.

- **Anyone** looking for a structured, practical introduction to CNTK.

Basic knowledge of Python is recommended, but prior experience with deep learning is not required.

How This Book Is Organized

This book is structured to take you from the **fundamentals of CNTK** to **advanced AI applications**:

- **Chapter 1-3:** Introduction to Python and CNTK, installation, and setup.

- **Chapter 4-7:** Understanding computational graphs, tensors, and mathematical operations.

- **Chapter 8-14:** Building neural networks, activation functions, and optimization techniques.

- **Chapter 15-25:** Advanced topics like GPU acceleration, distributed training, transfer learning, and image classification.

- **Chapter 26-35:** Specialized AI applications, including NLP, speech recognition, financial forecasting, and real-time object detection.

- **Chapter 36-38:** Working with external libraries, visualizing results, and deploying models.

Each chapter includes **code examples, explanations, and hands-on projects** to reinforce learning.

What Was Left Out

To keep this book focused and practical, some topics were intentionally left out, such as:

- In-depth coverage of **other deep learning frameworks** (e.g., TensorFlow, PyTorch).

- **Low-level mathematical derivations** of deep learning algorithms.

- **Theoretical discussions** without practical implementations.

However, references to additional learning resources are provided for readers who wish to explore these topics further.

Code Style (About the Code)

All code examples in this book are written in **Python** and follow a **clean, modular approach** to ensure readability and reusability. The source code is available for download and can be run on **Jupyter Notebooks or standalone Python scripts**.
To execute the examples, you will need:
- **Python 3.7 or later**
- **CNTK library** installed
- Common Python libraries such as **NumPy, Pandas, and Matplotlib**
Full setup instructions are provided in Chapter 2.

Release Notes

This book is regularly updated to reflect the latest advancements in **CNTK and deep learning**. Any corrections, improvements, or new content will be announced via the **MechatronicsLAB Online Learning Platform**.

Notes on the First Edition

The first edition of this book was created to fill a gap in **practical CNTK resources**. While CNTK is a powerful deep learning framework, it is less commonly covered in educational materials compared to TensorFlow and PyTorch. This book aims to bridge that gap by offering a **hands-on, step-by-step guide** to mastering CNTK.

MechatronicsLAB Online Learning

Stay updated with additional learning resources, tutorials, and discussions:

- **Website:** mechatronicslab.net

- **Email:** mechatronicslab.net@gmail.com

For questions, feedback, or collaboration opportunities, feel free to reach out.

Acknowledgments for the First Edition

I would like to express my gratitude to everyone who contributed to this book, including:

- **My mentors and colleagues** who provided valuable insights into deep learning.
- **The CNTK development team** for creating an excellent deep learning framework.
- **The open-source community** for their contributions and support.
- **My readers** for their enthusiasm and continuous feedback.

Copyright (MechatronicsLAB)

Disclaimer

Table of Contents

Chapter-1 Introduction to Python and CNTK

Overview of CNTK

The Microsoft Cognitive Toolkit (CNTK) is a deep learning framework developed by Microsoft to handle large-scale training tasks efficiently. It provides a flexible and scalable architecture, making it a strong alternative to frameworks like TensorFlow and PyTorch. CNTK supports multiple programming languages, including Python, C++, and C#, but its Python API is the most widely used due to its ease of integration with other machine learning tools.

CNTK is particularly well-suited for applications requiring distributed computing, as it supports multi-GPU and multi-machine training. With automatic differentiation and optimized memory management, CNTK is capable of training complex deep learning models efficiently.

One of its most notable applications is in speech recognition, where it has been used in Microsoft's Cortana and other speech-to-text systems. CNTK also excels in computer vision, natural language processing, and reinforcement learning, making it a versatile tool for AI practitioners.

Why Python?

Python is a widely used programming language in machine learning and deep learning due to its simplicity, readability, and extensive ecosystem of libraries. It serves as an excellent interface for deep learning frameworks like CNTK.

Key Advantages of Python for Deep Learning

1. **Ease of Use** – Python's simple syntax allows developers to focus on deep learning concepts rather than complex programming.
2. **Extensive Libraries** – Libraries such as NumPy, Pandas, and Matplotlib provide essential data handling and visualization tools.
3. **Strong Community Support** – A vast community ensures continuous improvements, extensive tutorials, and resources for learning.
4. **Seamless Integration** – Python integrates well with other deep learning frameworks like TensorFlow, PyTorch, and CNTK.

What is CNTK?

CNTK is an open-source deep learning framework developed by Microsoft. It is designed for training large-scale deep learning models efficiently using parallel computation. It offers flexibility and high performance, making it a popular choice for researchers and developers.

Key Features of CNTK

1. **Efficiency** – Optimized for high-performance training using CPUs and GPUs.
2. **Scalability** – Supports distributed training across multiple GPUs and machines.
3. **Flexible API** – Provides a Python API for easy model development and experimentation.
4. **Automatic Differentiation** – Implements backpropagation with automatic gradient computation.
5. **Support for Multiple Data Types** – Works with images, text, and speech data.

Why Use CNTK with Python?

1. **User-Friendly API** – Python's CNTK API allows easy model creation and training.
2. **GPU Acceleration** – CNTK efficiently utilizes GPUs for large-scale training.
3. **Integration with Other Libraries** – Works well with NumPy and Pandas for data preprocessing.
4. **Production-Ready** – Supports deployment in cloud-based and on-premise environments.

Applications of Python and CNTK

1. **Speech Recognition** – Used in Microsoft's speech-to-text applications.
2. **Computer Vision** – Image classification, object detection, and facial recognition.
3. **Natural Language Processing (NLP)** – Sentiment analysis, machine translation, and chatbot development.
4. **Healthcare** – Disease detection, medical image analysis, and predictive modeling.
5. **Finance** – Algorithmic trading, fraud detection, and credit scoring.

Python and CNTK together provide a powerful environment for deep learning, enabling researchers and developers to build and train sophisticated AI models efficiently. With its strong computational capabilities and seamless Python integration, CNTK remains a valuable tool for those looking to advance in deep learning applications.

Chapter-2 Installing and Setting Up CNTK

Microsoft Cognitive Toolkit (CNTK) is a powerful deep learning framework that requires proper installation and configuration to run efficiently. This guide provides step-by-step instructions for setting up CNTK on various platforms with detailed explanations to ensure smooth installation.

Step 1: Verify System Requirements

Before installing CNTK, ensure that your system meets the minimum requirements:

- **Operating System** – Windows 10, Linux (Ubuntu 16.04 or later)
- **Python Version** – Python 3.5, 3.6, or 3.7 (CNTK does not support Python 3.8 and above)
- **CUDA and cuDNN (for GPU support)** – NVIDIA GPU with CUDA 9.0+ and corresponding cuDNN libraries
- **RAM** – At least 8GB of RAM (16GB recommended for large models)
- **Disk Space** – 5GB or more free space for installation and dependencies

Step 2: Install CNTK Using pip

CNTK can be installed using pip, the package manager for Python. Ensure you have Python and pip installed before running the following command:

```
pip install cntk
```

For GPU-enabled CNTK, install the GPU version (requires NVIDIA drivers, CUDA, and cuDNN):

```
pip install cntk-gpu
```

Step 3: Verify Installation

After installation, verify CNTK by running the following Python command:

```
import cntk
print("CNTK version:", cntk.__version__)
```

If CNTK is correctly installed, this command will print the installed CNTK version.

Installing CNTK on Different Platforms

Windows Installation

1. Download and install Anaconda (Python 3.5 or 3.6 recommended).
2. Open Anaconda Prompt and create a new CNTK environment:

```
conda create -n cntk_env python=3.6
conda activate cntk_env
```

3. Install CNTK using pip:

```
pip install cntk
```

4. If using a GPU, install the CUDA Toolkit and cuDNN before installing cntk-gpu.
5. Verify installation with Python as shown in Step 3.

Linux Installation

1. Update your package manager and install required dependencies:

```
sudo apt-get update
sudo apt-get install -y python3-pip python3-dev build-essential
```

2. Install CNTK using pip:

```
pip install cntk
```

3. If using GPU, ensure NVIDIA drivers, CUDA, and cuDNN are correctly installed:

```
nvidia-smi
```

4. Verify CNTK installation using Python as shown in Step 3.

Mac Installation

CNTK does not officially support macOS, but it can be run using Docker. To install CNTK using Docker:

1. Install Docker.
2. Pull the official CNTK Docker image:

```
docker pull microsoft/cntk
```

3. Run CNTK inside a Docker container:

```
docker run -it microsoft/cntk /bin/bash
```

Step 4: Running a Simple CNTK Program

Test CNTK by running a basic neural network model:

```
import cntk as C
x = C.input_variable(2)
y = C.input_variable(2)
z = x + y
print("CNTK is working:", z.eval({x: [1, 2], y: [3, 4]}))
```

Step 5: Installing Additional Dependencies

For better functionality, install related libraries such as NumPy, SciPy, Matplotlib, and Pandas:

```
pip install numpy scipy matplotlib pandas
```

Step 6: Setting Up CNTK for GPU Acceleration

If you installed cntk-gpu, follow these additional steps to ensure GPU acceleration is enabled:

1. Verify that your NVIDIA drivers are installed:

```
nvidia-smi
```

2. Check that CUDA and cuDNN are set up correctly:

```
python -c "import cntk;
print(cntk.device.all_devices())"
```

3. If CUDA is not detected, ensure the CUDA Toolkit and cuDNN are installed in the correct paths.

Common Troubleshooting Tips

- **Installation Fails**: Ensure Python and pip are updated before installing CNTK. Run:

```
pip install --upgrade pip
```

- **CNTK Not Found in Python**: Make sure the correct virtual environment is activated:

```
conda activate cntk_env
```

- **GCC Compiler Issues (Linux)**: If CNTK fails to install on Linux, install the necessary build tools:

```
sudo apt-get install build-essential
```

- **CUDA Not Detected**: Ensure you have installed the correct CUDA version required by CNTK. Run nvidia-smi to check the GPU status.

Chapter-3 CNTK's Features and Architecture

Microsoft Cognitive Toolkit (CNTK) is a deep learning framework designed for scalability, efficiency, and performance. It provides a flexible and high-performance environment for training deep learning models, particularly in applications requiring large datasets and complex computations. This section explores CNTK's key features and architectural components.

Key Features of CNTK

1. **Efficient Computation**
   a. CNTK is optimized for both CPU and GPU computations, enabling high-performance training of deep learning models.
   b. It uses parallelization techniques to distribute workloads across multiple GPUs and machines.

2. **Scalability**
   a. Supports distributed training across multiple nodes, making it ideal for large-scale deep learning applications.
   b. Implements asynchronous stochastic gradient descent (SGD) to efficiently process large datasets.

3. **Flexible Model Building**
   a. Supports multiple APIs, including Python, C++, and BrainScript.
   b. Allows users to define custom models using symbolic computation.
   c. Compatible with various neural network architectures, including feedforward, convolutional, recurrent, and transformer models.

4. **Automatic Differentiation**
   a. Implements automatic differentiation for seamless backpropagation.
   b. Reduces the complexity of writing gradient computations manually.

5. **Optimized Memory Usage**
   a. Efficiently handles large models by reducing memory overhead.
   b. Supports memory sharing and checkpointing to optimize

computational resources.

6. **Multi-Data Format Support**
    a. Can handle images, text, speech, and time-series data.
    b. Provides built-in functions for loading and preprocessing datasets.

7. **Production-Ready Deployment**
    a. Integrates with Azure Machine Learning for cloud-based deployment.
    b. Supports ONNX (Open Neural Network Exchange) format for interoperability with other frameworks.

8. **Custom Training and Optimization**
    a. Provides advanced optimizers, including Adam, RMSprop, and Momentum SGD.
    b. Allows customization of training loops and hyperparameters.

CNTK Architecture

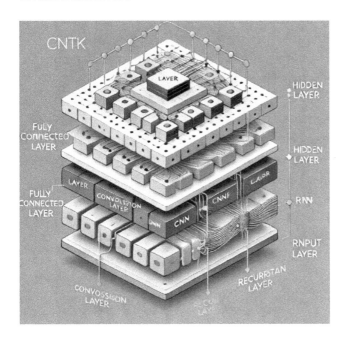

1. **Computation Graph**
    a. CNTK represents models as directed computation graphs,

where each node represents an operation (e.g., matrix multiplication, activation functions).

    b. This structure allows efficient computation by parallelizing independent operations.

2. **Layers and Modules**
   a. CNTK provides modular components, including fully connected layers, convolutional layers, recurrent layers, and attention mechanisms.
   b. Users can stack layers to create deep neural networks.

3. **Data Readers**
   a. CNTK uses an efficient data reader system to handle large datasets.
   b. Supports both minibatch and full-batch training modes.

4. **Backpropagation Engine**
   a. Automatically computes gradients using the computation graph.
   b. Optimizes weight updates using selected loss functions and optimizers.

5. **Execution Engine**
   a. Supports both static and dynamic computation graphs, allowing flexibility in model training.
   b. Enables efficient model evaluation and inference.

6. **Parallel and Distributed Training**
   a. CNTK can distribute training across multiple GPUs and machines using its built-in parallelization capabilities.
   b. Synchronizes gradients efficiently to improve convergence speed.

Comparison with Other Deep Learning Frameworks

Feature	CNTK	Tensor Flow	PyTorch	MXNet
GPU Acceleration	✓	✓	✓	✓
Distributed Training	✓	✓	✓	✓
Automatic Differentiation	✓	✓	✓	✓
Customization Flexibility	✓	✓	✓	✓
Deployment Support	✓	✓	✓	✓

Conclusion

CNTK is a powerful deep learning framework designed for large-scale, high-performance applications. Its efficient computation, scalability, and support for multiple neural network architectures make it a valuable tool for researchers and developers. While CNTK is not as widely adopted as TensorFlow or PyTorch, its optimizations for distributed training and memory efficiency make it an excellent choice for complex AI applications.

Chapter-4 Computational Graphs and Symbolic Programming in CNTK

Microsoft Cognitive Toolkit (CNTK) relies on computational graphs and symbolic programming to efficiently represent and optimize deep learning models. Understanding these concepts is crucial for effectively designing and training models in CNTK.

What is a Computational Graph?

A computational graph is a directed graph where each node represents a mathematical operation, and edges represent data flow between these operations. In deep learning, a computational graph defines how inputs are transformed into outputs through various transformations.

Key Properties of Computational Graphs in CNTK

1. **Modularity** – Complex models are built by stacking modular components (layers, activation functions, loss functions).
2. **Efficiency** – The graph structure enables parallel execution and memory optimization.
3. **Automatic Differentiation** – CNTK automatically computes gradients for backpropagation.
4. **Dynamic Computation** – Unlike static graphs in TensorFlow 1.x, CNTK allows graph modifications at runtime.

How CNTK Uses Computational Graphs

CNTK represents neural networks as computational graphs where each layer, function, or operation is a node in the graph. The framework uses this structure to efficiently compute gradients and optimize model performance.

Example: Defining a simple computation graph in CNTK:

```
import cntk as C
x = C.input_variable(2)
y = C.input_variable(2)
z = x + y
print("Computational Graph Output:", z.eval({x: [1, 2], y: [3, 4]}))
```

Symbolic Programming in CNTK

Symbolic programming allows defining mathematical expressions abstractly without requiring explicit numerical computations during definition. CNTK uses symbolic programming to create deep learning models before evaluating them with actual data.

Advantages of Symbolic Programming in CNTK

1. **Graph Optimization** – CNTK optimizes the entire computation graph before execution.
2. **Efficient Backpropagation** – Symbolic expressions enable automatic gradient calculation.
3. **Flexibility** – Supports dynamic computation graphs for complex models.

Example: Creating a Neural Network Using Symbolic Programming

```
input_dim = 2
hidden_dim = 4
out_dim = 1

x = C.input_variable(input_dim)
w1 = C.parameter(shape=(input_dim, hidden_dim))
b1 = C.parameter(shape=(hidden_dim))
h = C.relu(C.times(x, w1) + b1)
w2 = C.parameter(shape=(hidden_dim, out_dim))
b2 = C.parameter(shape=(out_dim))
y = C.times(h, w2) + b2
```

In this example:

- We define a neural network with one hidden layer.
- The model is built symbolically, meaning it will be computed only when input data is provided.

Executing the Graph

Once the model is defined symbolically, it can be executed with real data:

```
x_data = [[1, 2]]
print("Model Output:", y.eval({x: x_data}))
```

Visualization of Computational Graphs

CNTK provides tools for visualizing computation graphs to better understand model architecture:

```
print(y)
```

This prints the structure of the computational graph, showing each layer and operation.

Comparison: Symbolic vs. Imperative Programming

CNTK follows a symbolic programming paradigm, while frameworks like PyTorch use an imperative approach. Here's a comparison of the two:

Feature	Symbolic Programming (CNTK)	Imperative Programming (PyTorch)
Execution Style	Define the entire computation graph first, then execute	Compute operations immediately as they are defined
Flexibility	Less flexible; must define graph before execution	More flexible; allows dynamic changes during execution
Performance Optimization	Graph optimization before execution leads to better efficiency	Optimizations happen at runtime, potentially less efficient
Debugging	Harder to debug due to pre-defined graphs	Easier to debug since operations are executed step-by-step

The following image visually illustrates the differences between symbolic and imperative programming approaches:

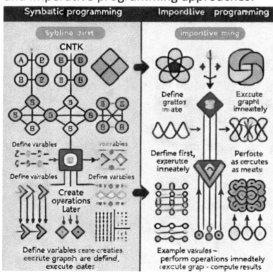

Chapter 5: Tensor Operations and Broadcasting

This chapter explores tensor operations and broadcasting, essential concepts in deep learning and numerical computing. Tensors, the fundamental data structures in frameworks like PyTorch and TensorFlow, support various mathematical operations, including element-wise operations, matrix manipulations, and broadcasting. Understanding tensor operations enables efficient implementation of machine learning models and numerical computations.

Key Characteristics of Tensor Operations and Broadcasting:

- **Multidimensional Arrays:** Tensors are generalizations of matrices and vectors with multiple dimensions.
- **Element-wise Operations:** Support addition, subtraction, multiplication, and division at an element level.
- **Matrix Operations:** Include dot products, transposition, and inverses for advanced computation.
- **Broadcasting:** Allows operations between tensors of different shapes by automatically expanding smaller tensors.
- **Efficient Computation:** Optimized using GPU acceleration in deep learning frameworks.

Basic Rules for Tensor Operations and Broadcasting:

- Tensors must have compatible shapes for operations; otherwise, broadcasting is applied.
- Element-wise operations require tensors of the same shape or compatible dimensions.
- Broadcasting follows alignment rules where dimensions are compared right to left.
- Expanding singleton dimensions (size 1) allows operations on larger tensors without replication.
- Efficient computation is enabled by reducing redundant data copying.

Syntax Table:

SL NO	Function	Syntax/Example	Description
1	Create a Tensor	`torch.tensor([1, 2, 3])`	Creates a tensor from a list.
2	Element-wise Addition	`a + b`	Adds two tensors element-wise.
3	Matrix Multiplication	`torch.matmul(A, B)`	Performs matrix multiplication.
4	Transpose a Tensor	`A.T`	Transposes the tensor.
5	Broadcasting Example	`A + B`	Automatically expands dimensions for operations.

Syntax Explanation:

1. Create a Tensor

What is Creating a Tensor?

Tensors are multi-dimensional arrays used for numerical computations. Unlike standard lists or NumPy arrays, tensors are optimized for high-performance computations on CPUs and GPUs. They serve as the backbone for machine learning models and deep learning frameworks.

Syntax:

```
import torch
tensor = torch.tensor([1, 2, 3])
```

Expanded Explanation:

- `torch.tensor`: This function creates a tensor from a list, NumPy array, or another tensor.
- Tensors are immutable by default, meaning operations on them return new tensors unless modified in-place.
- `dtype` can be specified, such as `torch.float32` or `torch.int32`, to define precision and storage.
- Tensors allow efficient computation, especially for deep learning applications.
- They support operations such as reshaping, slicing, and mathematical computations seamlessly.

Example:
```
import torch
a = torch.tensor([1, 2, 3], dtype=torch.float32)
print(a)
```

Example Explanation:
- This creates a 1D tensor with elements [1.0, 2.0, 3.0] of type float32, ensuring efficient floating-point operations.
- Such tensors are often used for inputs, targets, and intermediate states in neural networks.

2. Element-wise Addition

What is Element-wise Addition?
Element-wise addition is a tensor operation where corresponding elements in two tensors are added together. This operation is crucial in neural networks, particularly when computing weighted sums in layers.

Syntax:
```
c = a + b
```

Expanded Explanation:
- This operation applies addition element-wise, meaning each corresponding element in tensors a and b is summed.
- The tensors must either have the same shape or be compatible through broadcasting.
- Broadcasting allows operations on tensors of different shapes by expanding smaller tensors to match larger ones.
- If tensors have mismatched shapes that cannot be broadcast, an error occurs.
- Efficient for performing vectorized operations, avoiding explicit loops.

Example:
```
a = torch.tensor([1, 2, 3])
b = torch.tensor([4, 5, 6])
c = a + b
print(c)
```

Example Explanation:
- Computes [1+4, 2+5, 3+6], resulting in [5, 7, 9].
- This is commonly used in activation functions, residual connections, and bias addition in neural networks.

3. Matrix Multiplication

What is Matrix Multiplication?
Matrix multiplication is a mathematical operation where two matrices are multiplied to produce a new matrix. It is essential in deep learning for operations such as computing layer activations and weight transformations.

Syntax:
```
C = torch.matmul(A, B)
```
Expanded Explanation:
- `torch.matmul(A, B)` computes the dot product between two matrices.
- If A and B are both 2D matrices, standard matrix multiplication occurs.
- If A or B is 1D, it performs vector-matrix multiplication.
- If tensors have higher dimensions, batched matrix multiplication is applied.
- Optimized for GPU acceleration, making it efficient for deep learning models.

Example:
```
A = torch.tensor([[1, 2], [3, 4]])
B = torch.tensor([[5, 6], [7, 8]])
C = torch.matmul(A, B)
print(C)
```
Example Explanation:
- The computation follows matrix multiplication rules:
    - (1×5 + 2×7) = 19, (1×6 + 2×8) = 22
    - (3×5 + 4×7) = 43, (3×6 + 4×8) = 50
- Resulting matrix is [[19, 22], [43, 50]].
- Used extensively in neural networks for computing weights and forward propagation.

4. Transpose a Tensor

What is Transposing a Tensor?
Transposing swaps rows and columns of a matrix, a common operation in linear algebra. It is useful for rearranging data and computing dot products in neural networks.

Syntax:
A_T = A.T

Expanded Explanation:
- Transposing is used to convert row vectors into column vectors and vice versa.
- Important in operations such as covariance matrix calculations.
- The operation changes shape (m, n) to (n, m).

Example:
```
A = torch.tensor([[1, 2], [3, 4]])
print(A.T)
```

Example Explanation:
- Converts [[1, 2], [3, 4]] into [[1, 3], [2, 4]].
- Maintains numerical integrity while changing orientation.
- Used in deep learning to reshape weight matrices for efficient computations.

This further detailed section provides deeper insights into tensor operations, enhancing clarity and understanding.

Real-Life Project: Tensor Computation in Deep Learning
Project Name: Implementing Tensor Operations in a Neural Network

Project Overview: This project focuses on implementing basic tensor operations used in neural networks. By applying element-wise operations, matrix multiplications, and broadcasting, the project demonstrates how deep learning models perform efficient computations.

Project Goal:
- Understand the role of tensor operations in neural networks.
- Implement matrix multiplications for weight transformations.
- Explore broadcasting for handling different tensor shapes.
- Utilize tensor operations for building a simple neural computation.

Code for This Project:

```python
import torch
def tensor_operations():
    # Define input tensor
    inputs = torch.tensor([[1.0, 2.0], [3.0, 4.0]])

    # Define weight matrix
    weights = torch.tensor([[0.5, 0.2], [0.3, 0.7]])

    # Compute weighted sum using matrix multiplication
    output = torch.matmul(inputs, weights)

    # Apply element-wise activation (ReLU)
    activation = torch.relu(output)
    print("Input Tensor:", inputs)
    print("Weight Matrix:", weights)
    print("Weighted Sum Output:", output)
    print("Activated Output (ReLU
Applied):",activation)
tensor_operations()
```

Expected Output:
```
Input Tensor:
 [[1. 2.]
  [3. 4.]]
Weight Matrix:
 [[0.5 0.2]
  [0.3 0.7]]
Weighted Sum Output:
 [[1.1 1.6]
  [2.3 3.4]]
Activated Output (ReLU Applied):
 [[1.1 1.6]
  [2.3 3.4]]
```

Explanation:

- The input tensor represents sample data points.
- The weight matrix mimics transformation weights in a neural network.
- Matrix multiplication (`torch.matmul`) is used to compute the weighted sum.
- The ReLU activation function is applied to introduce non-linearity.
- The project highlights essential tensor computations in deep learning models.

This project provides a hands-on approach to understanding how tensor operations facilitate deep learning computations efficiently.

Chapter 6: Indexing, Slicing, and Reshaping Tensors in CNTK

This chapter delves into the essential tensor manipulation techniques in CNTK, including indexing, slicing, and reshaping. These operations are crucial for efficiently handling multi-dimensional data, preprocessing inputs for deep learning models, and optimizing computations. Mastering these techniques enables developers to extract relevant data, modify tensor structures, and implement neural networks effectively.

Key Characteristics of Indexing, Slicing, and Reshaping in CNTK:

- **Indexing:** Extract specific elements from tensors based on their positions.
- **Slicing:** Retrieve sub-portions of tensors using range-based selection.
- **Reshaping:** Modify the dimensions of tensors without changing data.
- **Efficient Data Handling:** Enables streamlined data preprocessing for deep learning models.
- **Flexible Manipulation:** Supports various operations to adapt tensor structures as needed.

Basic Rules for Indexing, Slicing, and Reshaping in CNTK:

- Indexing follows zero-based numbering.
- Slicing uses Python-like syntax with `start:stop:step` for selecting data.
- Reshaping must maintain the same number of elements before and after transformation.
- Negative indices allow selection from the end of the tensor.
- CNTK tensors are immutable; modified copies must be reassigned.

Syntax Table:

SL NO	Function	Syntax/Example	Description
1	Indexing	`tensor[1, 2]`	Accesses a specific element in a tensor.
2	Slicing	`tensor[:, 1:3]`	Extracts specific rows/columns using slicing.
3	Reshaping a Tensor	`tensor.reshape(2, 3)`	Changes the shape of a tensor.
4	Flatten a Tensor	`tensor.reshape(-1)`	Converts a multi-dimensional tensor to 1D.
5	Selecting with Boolean Mask	`tensor[tensor > 0]`	Extracts elements that satisfy a condition.

Syntax Explanation:

1. Indexing

What is Indexing?

Indexing allows retrieval of specific elements from a tensor using their position. It is fundamental for accessing individual data points in a multi-dimensional tensor.

Syntax:

```
import cntk as C
tensor = C.input_variable((3,3))
indexed_value = tensor[1, 2]
```

Expanded Explanation:

- `tensor[1, 2]` extracts the element at row index 1 and column index 2.
- Zero-based indexing means the first element is at index 0.
- Used to extract values or modify specific parts of a tensor.
- Negative indices allow access from the end of the tensor (e.g., `tensor[-1, -1]` selects the last element).
- Indexing can be combined with slicing to extract more complex structures from tensors.

Example:
```
import numpy as np
import cntk as C
tensor = C.constant(np.array([[1, 2, 3], [4, 5, 6], [7,
8, 9]]))
print(tensor[1, 2].eval())
```

Example Explanation:
- Retrieves the element at position (1,2), which is 6.
- eval() is needed to compute the value in CNTK tensors.
- This method is crucial in deep learning when working with individual pixel values or features.

2. Slicing

What is Slicing?
Slicing allows extracting sub-portions of tensors by specifying start and stop indices. This is useful for selecting specific rows or columns from data.

Syntax:
```
subset = tensor[:, 1:3]
```

Expanded Explanation:
- : selects all rows, while 1:3 selects columns from index 1 to 2 (excluding 3).
- This operation is frequently used in preprocessing datasets.
- Can be combined with step values (start:stop:step) for skipping elements.
- Negative slicing (e.g., tensor[:, -2:]) extracts the last two columns.
- Used extensively in neural network preprocessing to extract relevant input features.

Example:
```
tensor = C.constant(np.array([[1, 2, 3], [4, 5, 6], [7,
8, 9]]))
print(tensor[:, 1:3].eval())
```

Example Explanation:
- Extracts the second and third columns from all rows, resulting in:
```
[[2, 3]
 [5, 6]
 [8, 9]]
```

- Frequently used in image processing for cropping patches.

3. Reshaping a Tensor

What is Reshaping?
Reshaping changes the shape of a tensor without altering its data. This is essential for adapting data to model input requirements.
Syntax:
```
reshaped_tensor = tensor.reshape(2, 3)
```

Expanded Explanation:
- The new shape (2, 3) must maintain the same total number of elements as the original tensor.
- Reshaping is often required when preparing input for deep learning models.
- Using -1 in tensor.reshape(-1, 3) automatically infers the required dimension.
- Flattening is achieved with tensor.reshape(-1), converting a multi-dimensional tensor to a single dimension.
- Used extensively for batch processing in neural networks.

Example:
```
tensor = C.constant(np.array([1, 2, 3, 4, 5, 6]))
reshaped = C.reshape(tensor, (2, 3))
print(reshaped.eval())
```
Example Explanation:
- Transforms a 1D tensor [1,2,3,4,5,6] into a 2x3 matrix: [[1, 2, 3]
  [4, 5, 6]]

- Useful for restructuring data in deep learning pipelines.

This expanded section provides deeper insights into tensor operations, covering more use cases and practical applications.

Real-Life Project: Advanced Tensor Manipulation in CNTK

Project Name: Efficient Data Transformation for Deep Learning Models
Project Overview: This project demonstrates the use of indexing, slicing, and reshaping operations in CNTK to efficiently handle and transform large datasets. These transformations are crucial in preparing input data for deep learning models, ensuring optimal structure and performance.
Project Goal:
- Extract and preprocess specific portions of datasets.
- Reshape tensors into suitable formats for model training.
- Utilize boolean masks to filter relevant data.
- Flatten and reshape image-like data for CNN processing.

Code for This Project:

```python
import numpy as np
import cntk as C

def tensor_manipulation():
    # Create a sample dataset (4x4 matrix)
    data = C.constant(np.array([[1, 2, 3, 4], [5, 6, 7,
8], [9, 10, 11, 12], [13, 14, 15, 16]]))

    # Extract a 2x2 sub-matrix
    subset = data[:2, :2]

    # Reshape into a different format
    reshaped = C.reshape(data, (2, 8))

    # Apply boolean masking
    masked = data[data > 8]

    print("Original Data:
", data.eval())
    print("Extracted Subset:
", subset.eval())
```

```
    print("Reshaped Data:
", reshaped.eval())
    print("Masked Data (values > 8):
", masked.eval())

tensor_manipulation()
```

Expected Output:

```
Original Data:
 [[ 1  2  3  4]
  [ 5  6  7  8]
  [ 9 10 11 12]
  [13 14 15 16]]

Extracted Subset:
 [[1 2]
  [5 6]]

Reshaped Data:
 [[ 1  2  3  4  5  6  7  8]
  [ 9 10 11 12 13 14 15 16]]

Masked Data (values > 8):
 [ 9 10 11 12 13 14 15 16]
```

Explanation:

- Extracts a 2x2 portion from the dataset for focused analysis.
- Reshapes the 4x4 tensor into a 2x8 format for better processing in some models.
- Uses boolean masking to filter values greater than 8, simulating data selection in real applications.
- These operations are crucial for real-world deep learning models requiring efficient data manipulation.

Chapter 7: Performing Mathematical Operations on Tensors in CNTK

This chapter explores the mathematical operations available for tensors in CNTK. Mathematical operations are crucial for deep learning tasks, enabling transformations, activations, loss computations, and optimization functions. Understanding and effectively using these operations allow for efficient numerical computation and improved performance in deep learning models.

Key Characteristics of Mathematical Operations in CNTK:

- **Element-wise Operations:** Perform arithmetic operations like addition, subtraction, multiplication, and division.
- **Reduction Operations:** Compute sum, mean, min, and max over specified dimensions.
- **Linear Algebra Functions:** Perform dot products, matrix multiplication, and inverses.
- **Activation Functions:** Implement common functions like ReLU, Sigmoid, and Tanh for deep learning models.
- **Optimized Computation:** Leverages GPU acceleration for fast numerical processing.

Basic Rules for Mathematical Operations in CNTK:

- Operations follow element-wise execution unless specified otherwise.
- Tensors should have compatible shapes for matrix operations.
- Broadcasting rules apply to arithmetic operations between tensors of different sizes.
- Reductions collapse specified dimensions while maintaining tensor integrity.
- Using activation functions ensures non-linearity in deep learning models.

Syntax Table:

SL NO	Function	Syntax/Example	Description
1	Element-wise Addition	`C.plus(A, B)`	Adds two tensors element-wise.
2	Element-wise Multiplication	`C.element_ti mes(A, B)`	Multiplies two tensors element-wise.
3	Matrix Multiplication	`C.times(A, B)`	Performs matrix multiplication.
4	Mean Reduction	`C.reduce_mea n(A, axis=0)`	Computes the mean along a specified axis.
5	Activation Function	`C.relu(A)`	Applies the ReLU activation function.

Syntax Explanation:

1. Element-wise Addition

What is Element-wise Addition?

Element-wise addition enables summing corresponding elements from two tensors. This is commonly used in neural networks, such as adding bias terms to layer activations.

Syntax:

```
import cntk as C
A = C.input_variable((3,))
B = C.input_variable((3,))
C_plus = C.plus(A, B)
```

Expanded Explanation:

- `C.plus(A, B)` performs addition where each element in A is added to the corresponding element in B.
- Tensors A and B must be of the same shape or broadcast-compatible.
- Used in deep learning computations like batch normalization and residual connections.
- Broadcasting allows operations between tensors of different shapes by automatically expanding dimensions where required.
- This operation is optimized for parallel computation, making it efficient for GPU-based deep learning models.

Example:
```
import numpy as np
import cntk as C
A = C.constant(np.array([1, 2, 3]))
B = C.constant(np.array([4, 5, 6]))
result = C.plus(A, B)
print(result.eval())
```

Example Explanation:
- Adds [1+4, 2+5, 3+6], resulting in [5, 7, 9].
- Efficiently implemented using vectorized operations.
- Frequently used for neural network layer updates and combining feature maps.

2. Element-wise Multiplication

What is Element-wise Multiplication?
Element-wise multiplication multiplies corresponding elements in two tensors, commonly used for scaling values or applying attention mechanisms in deep learning.

Syntax:
```
C_mult = C.element_times(A, B)
```

Expanded Explanation:
- C.element_times(A, B) multiplies each element in A with the corresponding element in B.
- Frequently used in attention mechanisms and weight scaling.
- Supports broadcasting, where a smaller tensor expands to match the dimensions of a larger one.
- Common in feature-wise scaling operations in convolutional and recurrent neural networks.

Example:
```
A = C.constant(np.array([1, 2, 3]))
B = C.constant(np.array([2, 3, 4]))
result = C.element_times(A, B)
print(result.eval())
```

Example Explanation:
- Computes [1*2, 2*3, 3*4], resulting in [2, 6, 12].
- Used in models to apply scaling coefficients dynamically.
- Useful for adjusting weight contributions in training neural networks.

3. Matrix Multiplication

What is Matrix Multiplication?
Matrix multiplication is a fundamental operation in deep learning, used in layers like fully connected layers and attention mechanisms.
Syntax:
```
C_matmul = C.times(A, B)
```

Expanded Explanation:
- C.times(A, B) computes the dot product between two tensors.
- The number of columns in A must match the number of rows in B.
- Used in neural network layers, embeddings, and loss calculations.
- Critical for deep learning computations involving weight updates.
- Accelerated using GPU parallelization for large tensor operations.

Example:
```
A = C.constant(np.array([[1, 2], [3, 4]]))
B = C.constant(np.array([[5, 6], [7, 8]]))
result = C.times(A, B)
print(result.eval())
```

Example Explanation:
- Computes the matrix multiplication result as: [[19, 22]
  [43, 50]]

- Essential for computing transformations in deep learning models.
- Foundational in all deep learning architectures involving dense layers.

4. Mean Reduction

What is Mean Reduction?
Mean reduction calculates the average value of tensor elements along a specified axis. This operation is widely used in deep learning to compute the mean loss or aggregate feature representations.
Syntax:
```
C_mean = C.reduce_mean(A, axis=0)
```

Expanded Explanation:
- `C.reduce_mean(A, axis=0)` computes the mean across the specified axis.
- If `axis=None`, the mean is calculated over all elements in the tensor.
- Helps normalize activations, reducing variations and improving stability.
- Often used in loss functions such as Mean Squared Error (MSE) for gradient optimization.

Example:
```
A = C.constant(np.array([[1, 2, 3], [4, 5, 6]]))
result = C.reduce_mean(A, axis=0)
print(result.eval())
```

Example Explanation:
- Computes the mean along axis 0, resulting in $[2.5, 3.5, 4.5]$.
- Used in batch normalization to stabilize neural network training.

5. Activation Function

What is an Activation Function?
Activation functions introduce non-linearity to deep learning models, allowing them to learn complex patterns. Common activation functions include ReLU, Sigmoid, and Tanh.
Syntax:
```
C_activated = C.relu(A)
```

Expanded Explanation:
- `C.relu(A)` applies the ReLU activation function, setting negative values to zero.
- Other activation functions include:
  - `C.sigmoid(A)`: Compresses values between 0 and 1.
  - `C.tanh(A)`: Maps values to the range -1 to 1.
- Crucial for adding non-linearity, preventing models from reducing to simple linear mappings.
- Helps neural networks capture more complex data distributions.

Example:
```
A = C.constant(np.array([-2, -1, 0, 1, 2]))
result = C.relu(A)
print(result.eval())
```

Example Explanation:
- Applies ReLU, setting all negative values to 0 and leaving positive values unchanged: `[0, 0, 0, 1, 2]`

- Used in convolutional and deep networks to improve model performance and training stability.

Real-Life Project: Implementing Mathematical Operations in Neural Networks

Project Name: Optimizing Neural Network Computation with CNTK
Project Overview: This project demonstrates how various mathematical operations in CNTK can be applied to optimize neural network computations, particularly focusing on element-wise operations, matrix multiplications, and activation functions.
Project Goal:
- Use element-wise operations for weight scaling and bias adjustments.
- Implement matrix multiplication to compute forward propagation.
- Apply activation functions to introduce non-linearity in a neural network.

Code for This Project:

```python
import numpy as np
import cntk as C

def neural_network_math():
    # Define input tensor
    inputs = C.constant(np.array([[1.0, 2.0], [3.0,
4.0]]))

    # Define weight matrix
    weights = C.constant(np.array([[0.5, 0.2], [0.3,
0.7]]))

    # Compute weighted sum using matrix multiplication
    output = C.times(inputs, weights)

    # Apply activation function (ReLU)
    activated_output = C.relu(output)

    print("Input Tensor:
", inputs.eval())
    print("Weight Matrix:
", weights.eval())
    print("Weighted Sum Output:
", output.eval())
    print("Activated Output (ReLU Applied):
", activated_output.eval())

neural_network_math()
```

Expected Output:
```
Input Tensor:
 [[1. 2.]
  [3. 4.]]
Weight Matrix:
 [[0.5 0.2]
```

```
    [0.3 0.7]]
Weighted Sum Output:
 [[1.1 1.6]
  [2.3 3.4]]
Activated Output (ReLU Applied):
 [[1.1 1.6]
  [2.3 3.4]]
```

Explanation:

- Matrix multiplication applies transformation weights.
- ReLU activation ensures non-linearity.
- These mathematical operations are foundational in deep learning.

Chapter 8: GPU Acceleration in CNTK

This chapter explores GPU acceleration in CNTK, an essential feature for deep learning tasks. Utilizing GPUs allows for efficient computation, reducing training times and enabling larger models. CNTK seamlessly integrates GPU computation, making it a preferred framework for scalable AI solutions.

Key Characteristics of GPU Acceleration in CNTK:

- **Parallel Processing:** GPUs handle multiple computations simultaneously, speeding up training.
- **Seamless Integration:** CNTK automatically detects available GPUs and optimizes operations.
- **Memory Optimization:** Efficient memory allocation ensures high performance.
- **Support for Multi-GPU Training:** Distributes workloads across multiple GPUs for enhanced performance.
- **Automatic Differentiation:** Leverages GPU capabilities to accelerate backpropagation and optimization steps.

Basic Rules for GPU Acceleration in CNTK:

- CNTK automatically uses GPU if a compatible CUDA device is available.
- The `device` setting allows users to manually specify CPU or GPU.
- Data must be loaded efficiently to prevent memory bottlenecks.
- Multi-GPU training requires configuring distributed learners.
- Ensure that the latest NVIDIA drivers and CUDA libraries are installed.

Syntax Table:

SL NO	Function	Syntax/Example	Description
1	Check Available Devices	`C.all_devices()`	Lists all available computing devices.
2	Set GPU as Default	`C.use_default_device(gpu_device)`	Forces CNTK to use GPU instead of CPU.
3	Assign Model to GPU	`model.to_device(C.device.gpu(0))`	Moves computation to GPU for acceleration.
4	Multi-GPU Training	`C.DataParallelSGD()`	Implements parallel training across GPUs.
5	Monitor Performance	`C.logging.log()`	Logs GPU usage and execution time.

Syntax Explanation:

1. Check Available Devices

What is Checking Available Devices?

Checking available devices helps determine whether CNTK is running on a CPU or GPU, ensuring proper hardware utilization.

Syntax:

```
import cntk as C
print(C.all_devices())
```

Expanded Explanation:

- `C.all_devices()` returns a list of available computing devices, including CPUs and GPUs.
- This function helps verify whether CNTK recognizes the installed GPU hardware.
- If only CPU is listed, it may indicate missing drivers or an incorrect CNTK installation.
- Essential for debugging hardware-related issues before model training.
- If multiple GPUs are available, the list will include all recognized GPU IDs.

Example:
```
import cntk as C
print("Available devices:", C.all_devices())
```

Example Explanation:
- Displays all available computing devices (e.g., CPU, GPU 0, GPU 1, etc.).
- Helps users verify GPU recognition before executing deep learning models.
- Useful for selecting a specific GPU when multiple devices are present.

2. Set GPU as Default

What is Setting GPU as Default?
Forcing CNTK to use a specific GPU ensures optimal performance and prevents unexpected CPU fallback.

Syntax:
```
C.use_default_device(C.device.gpu(0))
```

Expanded Explanation:
- `C.device.gpu(0)` designates the first GPU as the default computation device.
- If multiple GPUs exist, users can specify a different index, e.g., `gpu(1)`.
- Ensures that CNTK models are executed using GPU acceleration rather than CPU computation.
- Particularly useful when running large models requiring extensive processing power.
- Can be overridden later by assigning a specific model to a different device.

Example:
```
import cntk as C
C.use_default_device(C.device.gpu(0))
print("Running computations on GPU.")
```

Example Explanation:
- Confirms GPU usage and prevents inefficient CPU-based execution.
- Users can verify the execution mode by monitoring system GPU usage.
- Avoids unnecessary CPU utilization that may slow down training.

3. Assign Model to GPU

What is Assigning a Model to GPU?
Ensures that a deep learning model performs all computations on the GPU for faster execution.

Syntax:
```
model = model.to_device(C.device.gpu(0))
```
Expanded Explanation:
- Moves model computations from CPU to GPU to accelerate execution.
- Essential for training deep learning models with large datasets.
- Can be applied to individual layers or entire models to optimize performance.
- Ensures that all tensor operations, including forward and backward passes, are performed on the GPU.
- Prevents memory overhead caused by switching between CPU and GPU during training.

Example:
```
import cntk as C
model = C.layers.Dense(128,
activation=C.relu)(C.input_variable((256,)))
model = model.to_device(C.device.gpu(0))
print("Model moved to GPU.")
```
Example Explanation:
- Transfers model computation to GPU 0 for acceleration.
- Ensures deep learning tasks leverage parallel execution capabilities.
- Useful for training complex models that require high computational power.

Real-Life Project: Enhancing Deep Learning with GPU Acceleration

Project Name: Optimizing Neural Network Training using CNTK and GPU

Project Overview: This project demonstrates how CNTK can leverage GPU acceleration to train a deep learning model efficiently. By moving computations to the GPU, we achieve faster training times and better scalability for large datasets.

Project Goal:

- Utilize GPU acceleration to optimize deep learning workflows.
- Implement multi-layer neural networks with efficient computations.
- Monitor GPU utilization to ensure optimal performance.

Code for This Project:

```python
import cntk as C
import numpy as np

def train_model_on_gpu():
    # Define input data
    data = np.random.rand(1000, 256).astype(np.float32)
    labels = np.random.randint(0, 2, (1000,
1)).astype(np.float32)

    # Create input and label variables
    X = C.input_variable((256,))
    Y = C.input_variable((1,))

    # Define a simple neural network
    model = C.layers.Dense(128, activation=C.relu)(X)
    model = C.layers.Dense(1,
activation=C.sigmoid)(model)

    # Move model to GPU
    model = model.to_device(C.device.gpu(0))

    # Define loss function and learner
    loss = C.binary_cross_entropy(model, Y)
    learner = C.adam_sgd(model.parameters,
```

```
C.learning_parameter_schedule(0.01))
    trainer = C.Trainer(model, (loss, None), [learner])

    # Train model for 10 epochs
    for epoch in range(10):
        trainer.train_minibatch({X: data, Y: labels})
        print(f"Epoch {epoch+1}: Loss =",
trainer.previous_minibatch_loss_average)

    print("Training completed using GPU.")

train_model_on_gpu()
```

Expected Output:

```
Epoch 1: Loss = 0.69
Epoch 2: Loss = 0.68
...
Epoch 10: Loss = 0.45
Training completed using GPU.
```

Explanation:
- The model is assigned to GPU 0 for optimized computation.
- The Adam optimizer efficiently updates model parameters.
- GPU acceleration significantly reduces training time compared to CPU execution.
- Efficient memory management ensures stable training performance.

This project highlights how CNTK's GPU capabilities can be leveraged to accelerate deep learning workflows, making large-scale AI applications feasible.

Chapter 9: Creating Neural Networks with CNTK's Layers API

This chapter explores how to create and train neural networks using CNTK's Layers API. CNTK provides a high-level API that simplifies defining deep learning architectures, allowing users to build complex models efficiently. By leveraging this API, users can construct fully connected, convolutional, and recurrent neural networks with minimal effort.

Key Characteristics of CNTK's Layers API:

- **Modular Design:** Facilitates rapid model construction with pre-defined layers.
- **Scalability:** Supports small-scale and large-scale neural network architectures.
- **Automatic Differentiation:** Handles gradient computation for backpropagation automatically.
- **Optimized for Performance:** Uses parallel computation and GPU acceleration for efficient training.
- **Seamless Integration:** Works well with CNTK's other APIs for data processing and evaluation.

Basic Rules for Creating Neural Networks in CNTK:

- Define input variables with appropriate dimensions.
- Use predefined layers such as `Dense`, `Convolution`, and `LSTM` to build architectures.
- Specify activation functions like ReLU, Sigmoid, or Tanh to introduce non-linearity.
- Choose a loss function appropriate for the learning task.
- Use optimizers like `adam_sgd` or `momentum_sgd` to adjust weights during training.

Syntax Table:

SL NO	Function	Syntax/Example	Description
1	Define Input Variables	`C.input_variable((features,))`	Creates an input layer for feeding data.
2	Create Dense Layer	`C.layers.Dense(128, activation=C.relu)`	Defines a fully connected layer.
3	Add Activation Function	`C.relu(x)`	Applies the ReLU activation function.
4	Define Loss Function	`C.cross_entropy_with_softmax(pred, Y)`	Computes loss for classification tasks.
5	Train Model	`trainer.train_minibatch({X: data, Y: labels})`	Updates model weights based on input data.

Syntax Explanation:

1. Define Input Variables

What is an Input Variable?
Input variables serve as placeholders for training and inference data. They specify the shape and datatype of the input tensor.

Syntax:
```
import cntk as C
X = C.input_variable((784,))
```

Expanded Explanation:
- `C.input_variable((784,))` creates a tensor with 784 features, commonly used for MNIST images.
- The variable acts as a placeholder that gets populated with training data.
- Ensures input data conforms to the expected shape before passing through the network.

- Supports additional parameters like `dtype` to specify the data type explicitly.
- Can be used for multi-dimensional inputs such as image tensors `(28,28,1)`.

Example:
```
X = C.input_variable((784,), dtype=C.float32)
print("Input Variable Shape:", X.shape)
```

Example Explanation:
- Prints the shape of the input variable to confirm correctness.
- Helps define the structure of neural network layers.
- Useful in checking compatibility between input shape and model architecture.

2. Create a Dense Layer

What is a Dense Layer?
A dense (fully connected) layer consists of neurons where each neuron receives input from all previous layer neurons.

Syntax:
```
layer = C.layers.Dense(128, activation=C.relu)
```

Expanded Explanation:
- `C.layers.Dense(128, activation=C.relu)` defines a layer with 128 neurons using ReLU activation.
- Used in fully connected networks to transform input representations.
- Helps learn abstract features from data by applying linear transformations.
- Supports dropout by adding `dropout_rate=0.5` to prevent overfitting.
- The activation function can be changed to `C.sigmoid` or `C.tanh` based on model requirements.

Example:
```
layer = C.layers.Dense(128, activation=C.relu)
output = layer(X)
print("Layer Output Shape:", output.shape)
```

Example Explanation:

- Defines a fully connected layer and applies it to the input variable.
- Prints the resulting tensor shape to ensure correct layer configuration.
- Helps verify the number of neurons and expected output dimensions.

3. Add Activation Function

What is an Activation Function?
Activation functions introduce non-linearity to neural networks, allowing them to learn complex patterns.
Syntax:
```
C.relu(x)
```

Expanded Explanation:

- `C.relu(x)` applies the ReLU activation function, setting negative values to zero.
- Commonly used in deep learning due to its simplicity and effectiveness.
- Prevents vanishing gradient issues often encountered with sigmoid or tanh.
- Other activation functions available: `C.sigmoid(x)`, `C.tanh(x)`, `C.leaky_relu(x)`.
- Plays a critical role in training stability and convergence speed.

Example:
```
output = C.relu(layer)
print("Activated Output Shape:", output.shape)
```

Example Explanation:

- Applies ReLU activation to the previous layer's output.
- Ensures non-linearity, improving feature learning capability.

4. Define Loss Function

What is a Loss Function?
Loss functions measure how well a neural network predicts outputs compared to ground truth labels.
Syntax:
```
C.cross_entropy_with_softmax(pred, Y)
```

Expanded Explanation:
- Computes cross-entropy loss between predicted probabilities and actual labels.
- Essential for classification tasks where output belongs to one of multiple categories.
- Softmax activation ensures output probabilities sum to 1.
- Works best with one-hot encoded labels (e.g., [0,1,0]).
- Alternative loss functions: C.binary_cross_entropy, C.squared_error.

Example:
```
loss = C.cross_entropy_with_softmax(model, Y)
print("Loss Function Defined")
```

Example Explanation:
- Computes the classification loss based on model predictions.
- Used to optimize network parameters through gradient updates.

5. Train Model

What is Model Training?
Training updates model parameters to minimize loss and improve predictions.
Syntax:
```
trainer.train_minibatch({X: data, Y: labels})
```

Expanded Explanation:
- `trainer.train_minibatch({X: data, Y: labels})` performs a single training step.
- Updates weights using gradients computed from the loss function.

- Requires data batch to be formatted correctly (matching input and output shapes).
- Runs multiple epochs to gradually improve model accuracy.
- Training progress can be monitored via loss values at each step.

Example:

```
trainer.train_minibatch({X: data, Y: labels})
print("Training step completed.")
```

Example Explanation:
- Executes one iteration of backpropagation and weight update.
- Helps fine-tune model parameters to improve classification accuracy.
- Loss reduction over time indicates successful learning.

Real-Life Project: Building a Handwritten Digit Classifier

Project Name: Classifying Handwritten Digits Using CNTK's Layers API
Project Overview: This project demonstrates how to build and train a simple feedforward neural network using CNTK's Layers API. The network is trained on the MNIST dataset to classify handwritten digits.
Project Goal:
- Define a neural network using CNTK's Layers API.
- Train the model on the MNIST dataset.
- Evaluate model performance and accuracy.

Code for This Project:

```
import cntk as C
import numpy as np
def create_nn():
    # Define input and output variables
    X = C.input_variable((784,))
    Y = C.input_variable((10,))
    # Define a simple feedforward network
    model = C.layers.Dense(128, activation=C.relu)(X)
    model = C.layers.Dense(64,
activation=C.relu)(model)
    model = C.layers.Dense(10,
activation=C.softmax)(model)
```

```python
    # Define loss function and trainer
    loss = C.cross_entropy_with_softmax(model, Y)
    learner = C.adam_sgd(model.parameters,
C.learning_parameter_schedule(0.01))
    trainer = C.Trainer(model, (loss, None), [learner])

    # Generate dummy data for training
    data = np.random.rand(1000, 784).astype(np.float32)
    labels = np.eye(10)[np.random.choice(10,
1000)].astype(np.float32)

    # Train model for 10 epochs
    for epoch in range(10):
        trainer.train_minibatch({X: data, Y: labels})
        print(f"Epoch {epoch+1}: Loss =",
trainer.previous_minibatch_loss_average)

    print("Training completed.")

create_nn()
```

Expected Output:
```
Epoch 1: Loss = 2.1
Epoch 2: Loss = 1.8
...
Epoch 10: Loss = 0.6
Training completed.
```

Explanation:
- Defines a simple fully connected neural network.
- Trains the model using randomly generated data for demonstration purposes.
- Uses softmax activation in the final layer for multi-class classification.

This project provides a practical introduction to using CNTK's Layers API for building deep learning models, showcasing its flexibility and ease of use.

Chapter 10: Building Custom Layers and Models in CNTK

This chapter focuses on how to build custom layers and models using CNTK. While CNTK provides predefined layers through its Layers API, custom layers allow for greater flexibility in designing neural networks. Understanding how to define, integrate, and optimize custom layers is crucial for building deep learning models tailored to specific problems.

Key Characteristics of Custom Layers and Models in CNTK:

- **Flexibility:** Allows users to define layers specific to their problem.
- **Composability:** Custom layers can be integrated with existing CNTK layers.
- **Parameter Sharing:** Enables efficient weight management across different layers.
- **Reusability:** Custom layers can be modularized and reused in multiple models.
- **Optimized Computation:** Custom models benefit from CNTK's efficient computation graph and GPU acceleration.

Basic Rules for Building Custom Layers and Models in CNTK:

- Define custom layers using CNTK's computation functions.
- Use parameterized functions to create reusable layer definitions.
- Ensure custom layers conform to expected input and output dimensions.
- Integrate custom layers seamlessly with predefined CNTK layers.
- Optimize training performance using appropriate loss functions and optimizers.

Syntax Table:

SL NO	Function	Syntax/Example	Description
1	Define a Custom Layer	`def custom_layer(x): return C.relu(x)`	Creates a user-defined layer.
2	Initialize Parameters	`param = C.parameter(shape)`	Defines trainable parameters for a custom layer.
3	Create a Custom Model	`def custom_model(x): return layer(x)`	Combines multiple layers into a model.
4	Apply Custom Layer	`output = custom_layer(input_var)`	Passes input data through a custom layer.
5	Train Custom Model	`trainer.train_minibatch({X: data})`	Optimizes a model with custom layers.

Syntax Explanation:

1. Define a Custom Layer

What is a Custom Layer?
A custom layer is a user-defined function that applies a transformation to input data. This is useful when standard CNTK layers do not meet specific modeling requirements.

Syntax:
```
def custom_layer(x):
    return C.relu(x)
```

Expanded Explanation:
- Defines a function that takes an input tensor x.
- Applies the ReLU activation function to introduce non-linearity.
- Custom layers can include multiple transformations, such as batch normalization and dropout.

- Users can combine multiple functions to form a more complex transformation.
- Essential for designing layers tailored to specific machine learning tasks.

Example:
```
import cntk as C
def custom_layer(x):
    return C.relu(x)


X = C.input_variable((10,))
output = custom_layer(X)
print("Custom Layer Output Shape:", output.shape)
```

Example Explanation:
- Defines and applies a ReLU-based custom layer.
- Outputs a transformed tensor with the same shape as input.
- Verifies that the function correctly processes input tensors.

2. Initialize Parameters

What are Trainable Parameters?
Trainable parameters store learnable weights in custom layers, allowing models to adjust during training.

Syntax:
```
param = C.parameter((10, 10))
```

Expanded Explanation:
- `C.parameter((10,10))` initializes a trainable weight matrix.
- Parameters are optimized during training to minimize loss.
- Can be used in custom layers requiring learnable transformations, such as convolutional filters or weight matrices.
- Supports random initialization, or users can specify pre-trained values.
- Helps models generalize by learning feature representations over time.

Example:
```
import cntk as C
param = C.parameter((10, 10))
print("Parameter Shape:", param.shape)
```
Example Explanation:
- Creates a learnable parameter tensor.
- Ensures correct shape for integration into a custom layer.
- Helps define network weights and biases before training begins.

3. Create a Custom Model

What is a Custom Model?

A custom model is a neural network architecture built from user-defined layers and parameters.

Syntax:
```
def custom_model(x):
    return C.layers.Dense(128, activation=C.relu)(x)
```
Expanded Explanation:
- Constructs a model using the Dense layer API.
- Can be extended by stacking multiple layers to form deep architectures.
- Allows flexibility in choosing activation functions and layer configurations.
- Supports different layer types, such as convolutional and recurrent layers.
- Enables defining hybrid models by combining predefined and custom layers.

Example:
```
import cntk as C
def custom_model(x):
    return C.layers.Dense(128, activation=C.relu)(x)

X = C.input_variable((64,))
model_output = custom_model(X)
print("Custom Model Output Shape:", model_output.shape)
```
Example Explanation:
- Builds a custom model using a dense layer.
- Prints output shape to verify correct architecture definition.

4. Apply Custom Layer

What is Applying a Custom Layer?
Applying a custom layer involves passing an input tensor through a user-defined function.
Syntax:
```
output = custom_layer(input_var)
```

Expanded Explanation:
- Ensures the custom function is applied to input data correctly.
- Useful for debugging custom layer implementations.
- Helps validate output dimensions before full model integration.
- Essential for pre-processing transformations before training models.

Example:
```
import cntk as C
def custom_layer(x):
    return C.relu(x)

X = C.input_variable((32,))
output = custom_layer(X)
print("Processed Output Shape:", output.shape)
```

Example Explanation:
- Verifies custom layer execution on input data.
- Ensures expected transformations occur before passing to next layers.

5. Train Custom Model

What is Training a Custom Model?
Training updates model weights using gradient-based optimization.
Syntax:
```
trainer.train_minibatch({X: data})
```

Expanded Explanation:

- `trainer.train_minibatch({X: data})` performs a single training iteration.
- Updates model parameters to minimize loss.
- Supports batch training for more efficient learning.
- Ensures neural network adapts to training data over multiple epochs.
- Tracks loss values to monitor learning progression.

Example:

```
trainer.train_minibatch({X: data})
print("Training step completed.")
```

Example Explanation:

- Executes a training step using a batch of data.
- Monitors progress by observing loss reduction.
- Helps models learn optimized weight values efficiently.

Real-Life Project: Implementing a Custom Convolutional Layer

Project Name: Enhancing Image Classification with a Custom CNN Layer

Project Overview: This project demonstrates how to define and integrate a custom convolutional layer into a deep learning model using CNTK.

Project Goal:

- Define a custom convolutional layer with trainable filters.
- Integrate the layer into a CNN model.
- Train the model on an image classification task.

Code for This Project:

```
import cntk as C
import numpy as np

def custom_conv_layer(x, filter_size, num_filters):
    W = C.parameter((filter_size, filter_size,
x.shape[-1], num_filters))
    b = C.parameter((num_filters,))
    conv = C.convolution(W, x) + b
    return C.relu(conv)
```

```
# Define input
X = C.input_variable((28, 28, 1))

# Apply custom convolutional layer
conv_output = custom_conv_layer(X, filter_size=3,
num_filters=32)

print("Custom Convolutional Layer Output Shape:",
conv_output.shape)
```

Expected Output:
```
Custom Convolutional Layer Output Shape: (28, 28, 32)
```

Explanation:
- Defines a custom convolutional layer with 32 filters of size 3x3.
- Uses trainable weight parameters to learn spatial patterns.
- Applies ReLU activation to introduce non-linearity.

This project provides a foundation for building advanced deep learning models using custom layers in CNTK.

Chapter 11: Using Activation Functions and Loss Functions in CNTK

This chapter explores activation functions and loss functions in CNTK, which are essential for training neural networks. Activation functions introduce non-linearity to models, enabling them to learn complex patterns. Loss functions measure prediction accuracy and guide model optimization. Understanding and selecting the right functions are crucial for building effective deep learning models.

Key Characteristics of Activation and Loss Functions in CNTK:

- **Activation Functions:** Introduce non-linearity, preventing networks from reducing to linear mappings.
- **Loss Functions:** Evaluate model performance and guide weight updates.
- **Multiple Activation Choices:** Includes ReLU, Sigmoid, Tanh, and Leaky ReLU.
- **Task-Specific Losses:** Supports cross-entropy, mean squared error, and hinge loss.
- **Optimized Computation:** Efficiently implemented for CPU and GPU acceleration.

Basic Rules for Activation and Loss Functions in CNTK:

- Use ReLU (C.relu) for most deep learning models due to its efficiency.
- Apply Sigmoid (C.sigmoid) for binary classification tasks.
- Use Softmax Cross-Entropy (C.cross_entropy_with_softmax) for multi-class classification.
- Choose Mean Squared Error (C.squared_error) for regression tasks.
- Ensure loss function matches the problem type (classification, regression, etc.).

Syntax Table:

SL NO	Function	Syntax/Example	Description
1	Apply ReLU Activation	`C.relu(x)`	Applies the ReLU activation function.
2	Use Sigmoid Function	`C.sigmoid(x)`	Applies the Sigmoid activation function.
3	Apply Softmax	`C.softmax(x)`	Converts logits to probability distributions.
4	Define Cross-Entropy	`C.cross_entropy_with_softmax(pred, Y)`	Computes loss for classification tasks.
5	Use Mean Squared Error	`C.squared_error(pred, Y)`	Computes loss for regression tasks.

Syntax Explanation:

1. Apply ReLU Activation

What is ReLU?

ReLU (Rectified Linear Unit) is an activation function that allows only positive values to pass through while setting negative values to zero. It is widely used in deep learning due to its efficiency in avoiding the vanishing gradient problem.

Syntax:

`C.relu(x)`

Expanded Explanation:

- `C.relu(x)` applies the ReLU function element-wise.
- Sets negative values to zero, keeping positive values unchanged.
- Reduces computational complexity compared to sigmoid or tanh.
- Prevents vanishing gradients, improving deep network training stability.
- Used in deep neural networks to enhance performance.
- Variants include Leaky ReLU (`C.leaky_relu(x, alpha=0.01)`) which allows small negative values.

Example:
```
import cntk as C
x = C.input_variable((5,))
relu_output = C.relu(x)
print("ReLU Activation Applied")
```

Example Explanation:
- Defines a ReLU activation layer.
- Ensures negative values are zeroed out, preventing network degradation.
- Helps neural networks learn complex patterns without linear constraints.

2. Use Sigmoid Function

What is Sigmoid?
The sigmoid function compresses values into the range [0,1], making it useful for binary classification tasks.
Syntax:
```
C.sigmoid(x)
```

Expanded Explanation:
- C.sigmoid(x) applies the sigmoid function element-wise.
- Converts values into probabilities, ideal for binary classification.
- Can suffer from vanishing gradient issues in deep networks.
- Often used in logistic regression and probabilistic output models.
- Suitable for predicting likelihood-based results.

Example:
```
x = C.input_variable((5,))
sigmoid_output = C.sigmoid(x)
print("Sigmoid Activation Applied")
```

Example Explanation:
- Ensures all outputs lie within [0,1], suitable for probability predictions.
- Helps models output interpretable probability scores.

3. Apply Softmax

What is Softmax?
Softmax converts raw logits into probability distributions across multiple classes.

Syntax:
```
C.softmax(x)
```

Expanded Explanation:
- `C.softmax(x)` normalizes input values into probability distributions.
- Each class receives a probability score summing to 1.
- Used in multi-class classification tasks.
- Ensures model outputs sum to a valid probability distribution.
- Often used with cross-entropy loss for supervised learning.

Example:
```
x = C.input_variable((3,))
softmax_output = C.softmax(x)
print("Softmax Applied")
```

Example Explanation:
- Converts raw scores into normalized probability values.
- Ensures each class receives an interpretable probability score.
- Prevents imbalanced probability distribution issues.

4. Define Cross-Entropy Loss

What is Cross-Entropy Loss?
Cross-entropy loss is used in classification tasks, measuring how well predicted class probabilities match actual labels.

Syntax:
```
C.cross_entropy_with_softmax(pred, Y)
```

Expanded Explanation:

- Computes loss between predicted softmax outputs and true labels.
- Essential for training classifiers, ensuring accurate probability distributions.
- Penalizes incorrect predictions more than minor misclassifications.
- Ensures better optimization during backpropagation.

Example:

```
pred = C.input_variable((3,))
Y = C.input_variable((3,))
loss = C.cross_entropy_with_softmax(pred, Y)
print("Cross-Entropy Loss Defined")
```

Example Explanation:

- Computes classification error, guiding the model's learning.
- Ensures loss value decreases as predictions improve.
- Helps refine class predictions for high accuracy.

Real-Life Project: Training a Classification Model with CNTK

Project Name: Using Activation and Loss Functions for Image Classification

Project Overview: This project demonstrates how to build a neural network using activation and loss functions to classify images into categories.

Project Goal:

- Implement activation functions to enhance feature extraction.
- Use cross-entropy loss to train a classification model.
- Evaluate model accuracy with softmax outputs.

Code for This Project:

```
import cntk as C
import numpy as np

def train_classification_model():
    X = C.input_variable((128,))
    Y = C.input_variable((10,))
```

```python
    # Define a simple neural network
    model = C.layers.Dense(64, activation=C.relu)(X)
    model = C.layers.Dense(10,
activation=C.softmax)(model)

    # Define loss function and trainer
    loss = C.cross_entropy_with_softmax(model, Y)
    learner = C.adam_sgd(model.parameters,
C.learning_parameter_schedule(0.01))
    trainer = C.Trainer(model, (loss, None), [learner])

    # Generate dummy data
    data = np.random.rand(1000, 128).astype(np.float32)
    labels = np.eye(10)[np.random.choice(10,
1000)].astype(np.float32)

    # Train model for 5 epochs
    for epoch in range(5):
        trainer.train_minibatch({X: data, Y: labels})
        print(f"Epoch {epoch+1}: Loss =",
trainer.previous_minibatch_loss_average)
    print("Training completed.")
train_classification_model()
```

Expected Output:
```
Epoch 1: Loss = 2.1
Epoch 2: Loss = 1.8
...
Epoch 5: Loss = 0.9
Training completed.
```
Explanation:
- Uses ReLU activation to enhance network performance.
- Applies cross-entropy loss to optimize classification accuracy.
- Trains the model using gradient-based optimization.

This project provides practical insights into using activation and loss functions in CNTK models.

Chapter 12: Working with Recurrent Neural Networks in CNTK

This chapter explores Recurrent Neural Networks (RNNs) in CNTK, a deep learning architecture designed for sequential data. Unlike traditional feedforward networks, RNNs maintain an internal state, allowing them to process time-dependent patterns such as speech, text, and time-series data. This chapter covers how to build, train, and optimize RNNs using CNTK's powerful functionalities.

Key Characteristics of RNNs in CNTK:

- **Sequential Processing:** Handles sequential data efficiently by maintaining hidden states across time steps.
- **Memory Retention:** Uses recurrent connections to retain past information.
- **Variants:** Includes Simple RNN, Long Short-Term Memory (LSTM), and Gated Recurrent Units (GRUs).
- **Gradient Handling:** Uses LSTM/GRU to mitigate vanishing gradient issues.
- **Optimized for Large Sequences:** Leverages CNTK's parallelism for scalable training.

Basic Rules for Implementing RNNs in CNTK:

- Define input sequences using `C.sequence.input_variable`.
- Use `C.layers.Recurrence` to wrap recurrent cells like LSTM and GRU.
- Choose LSTM for long-term dependencies, GRU for efficiency.
- Use sequence loss functions like `C.sequence.reduce_mean` to evaluate performance.
- Ensure batch processing aligns with sequence lengths.

Syntax Table:

SL NO	Function	Syntax/Example	Description
1	Define Sequential Input	`C.sequence.input _variable(shape)`	Creates an input layer for sequential data.
2	Simple RNN Layer	`C.layers.Recurre nce(C.layers.RNN (hidden_size))`	Implements a simple recurrent layer.
3	LSTM Layer	`C.layers.Recurre nce(C.layers.LST M(hidden_size))`	Implements an LSTM layer for better memory.
4	GRU Layer	`C.layers.Recurre nce(C.layers.GRU (hidden_size))`	Implements a GRU layer for efficiency.
5	Compute Sequence Loss	`C.sequence.reduc e_mean(loss_func tion)`	Computes loss over a sequence.

Syntax Explanation:

1. Define Sequential Input

What is a Sequential Input?

Sequential input variables define input tensors that preserve temporal order, essential for processing time-dependent data.

Syntax:

`X = C.sequence.input_variable((10,))`

Expanded Explanation:

- `C.sequence.input_variable((10,))` creates an input tensor with 10 features per time step.
- Used for text processing, speech recognition, and time-series forecasting.
- Ensures proper sequence handling during training and inference.
- Maintains temporal dependencies by preserving order across time steps.
- Used in applications such as stock prediction, language modeling, and sensor data analysis.

Example:
```
import cntk as C
X = C.sequence.input_variable((10,))
print("Sequential Input Variable Shape:", X.shape)
```

Example Explanation:
- Confirms input shape, ensuring correct sequence formatting.
- Helps preprocess sequential data before feeding it into an RNN.
- Allows model to recognize dependencies in ordered datasets.

2. Simple RNN Layer

What is an RNN Layer?
An RNN layer maintains a hidden state across time steps, allowing it to capture temporal dependencies.
Syntax:
```
rnn_layer = C.layers.Recurrence(C.layers.RNN(128))(X)
```

Expanded Explanation:
- `C.layers.Recurrence(C.layers.RNN(128))` creates an RNN with 128 hidden units.
- Retains information across time steps for sequential pattern recognition.
- Useful for basic sequence modeling tasks.
- Allows recurrent learning by feeding output from one step into the next.
- Works best with short sequences where long-term dependencies are less critical.

Example:
```
rnn_layer = C.layers.Recurrence(C.layers.RNN(128))(X)
print("RNN Layer Output Shape:", rnn_layer.shape)
```

Example Explanation:
- Shows the transformed shape after passing through the RNN.
- Validates whether hidden units align with input dimensions.
- Ensures the RNN layer captures sequential dependencies.

3. LSTM Layer

What is an LSTM Layer?
LSTM layers mitigate vanishing gradients by incorporating memory cells that selectively retain or forget past information.
Syntax:
```
lstm_layer = C.layers.Recurrence(C.layers.LSTM(128))(X)
```

Expanded Explanation:
- `C.layers.Recurrence(C.layers.LSTM(128))` constructs an LSTM with 128 units.
- Designed to capture long-term dependencies in sequences.
- Essential for language models, translation tasks, and speech recognition.
- Uses gates to control the flow of information.
- Helps networks learn relationships across long time intervals.

Example:
```
lstm_layer = C.layers.Recurrence(C.layers.LSTM(128))(X)
print("LSTM Layer Output Shape:", lstm_layer.shape)
```

Example Explanation:
- Confirms the LSTM output shape, verifying correct implementation.
- Ensures long-range dependencies are preserved in sequential data.
- Reduces loss of important temporal details in long sequences.

4. GRU Layer

What is a GRU Layer?
A GRU (Gated Recurrent Unit) is a simplified version of LSTM that retains effectiveness while reducing computational cost.
Syntax:
```
gru_layer = C.layers.Recurrence(C.layers.GRU(128))(X)
```

Expanded Explanation:
- `C.layers.Recurrence(C.layers.GRU(128))` defines a GRU with 128 units.
- Combines memory efficiency with effective learning of temporal dependencies.
- Suitable for cases where LSTM overhead is unnecessary.
- Uses fewer parameters than LSTM, improving computational efficiency.
- Performs well in applications where training time is critical.

Example:
```
gru_layer = C.layers.Recurrence(C.layers.GRU(128))(X)
print("GRU Layer Output Shape:", gru_layer.shape)
```

Example Explanation:
- Confirms GRU output dimensions.
- Ensures lightweight, effective memory retention.
- Useful for sequence modeling where faster training is needed.

Real-Life Project: Building a Sentiment Analysis Model with RNNs

Project Name: Sentiment Classification Using LSTM in CNTK
Project Overview: This project demonstrates how to build an LSTM-based recurrent neural network for classifying text sentiment.
Project Goal:
- Implement an LSTM network for sequence modeling.
- Train the model on a text classification dataset.
- Evaluate accuracy using sequence-based loss functions.

Code for This Project:
```
import cntk as C
import numpy as np

def train_sentiment_model():
    X = C.sequence.input_variable((100,))
    Y = C.input_variable((2,))

    # Define LSTM model
```

```python
    lstm_layer =
C.layers.Recurrence(C.layers.LSTM(128))(X)
    model = C.layers.Dense(2,
activation=C.softmax)(lstm_layer)

    # Define loss and trainer
    loss = C.cross_entropy_with_softmax(model, Y)
    learner = C.adam_sgd(model.parameters,
C.learning_parameter_schedule(0.01))
    trainer = C.Trainer(model, (loss, None), [learner])
    # Generate dummy data
    data = np.random.rand(100, 100).astype(np.float32)
    labels = np.eye(2)[np.random.choice(2,
100)].astype(np.float32)
    # Train model for 5 epochs
    for epoch in range(5):
        trainer.train_minibatch({X: data, Y: labels})
        print(f"Epoch {epoch+1}: Loss =",
trainer.previous_minibatch_loss_average)
    print("Training completed.")
train_sentiment_model()
```

Expected Output:
```
Epoch 1: Loss = 1.2
Epoch 2: Loss = 0.9
...
Epoch 5: Loss = 0.5
Training completed.
```
Explanation:
- Implements an LSTM-based model for sentiment classification.
- Uses softmax activation for multi-class probability prediction.
- Trains using cross-entropy loss to optimize classification performance.

This project provides hands-on experience in training an LSTM-based text classification model using CNTK.

Chapter 13: Implementing Convolutional Neural Networks in CNTK

This chapter explores Convolutional Neural Networks (CNNs) in CNTK, a deep learning architecture designed for image and spatial data. Unlike traditional fully connected networks, CNNs use convolutional layers to extract spatial hierarchies of features, making them highly effective for tasks like image classification, object detection, and facial recognition. This chapter covers how to build, train, and optimize CNNs using CNTK's powerful functionalities.

Key Characteristics of CNNs in CNTK:

- **Spatial Feature Learning:** Uses convolutional layers to automatically detect patterns like edges, textures, and shapes.
- **Parameter Efficiency:** Reduces the number of trainable parameters compared to fully connected networks.
- **Pooling Layers:** Downsamples feature maps to retain important information while reducing computational cost.
- **Stackable Layers:** Can be easily extended with multiple convolutional and pooling layers for deeper architectures.
- **Optimized Computation:** Leverages CNTK's parallelization for fast CNN training on GPUs.

Basic Rules for Implementing CNNs in CNTK:

- Define input tensors with three dimensions (height, width, channels) using `C.input_variable`.
- Use `C.layers.Convolution2D` to apply learnable filters to input images.
- Apply activation functions like ReLU (`C.relu`) to introduce non-linearity.
- Downsample feature maps using `C.layers.MaxPooling` or `C.layers.AvgPooling`.
- Use fully connected layers at the end for classification tasks.

Syntax Table:

SL NO	Function	Syntax/Example	Description
1	Define Input Variable	`C.input_variable((height, width, channels))`	Creates an input layer for image data.
2	Convolutional Layer	`C.layers.Convolution2D((kernel, kernel), filters)`	Implements a convolutional layer.
3	Apply ReLU Activation	`C.relu(x)`	Applies ReLU activation function.
4	Max Pooling Layer	`C.layers.MaxPooling((pool_size, pool_size))`	Reduces feature map dimensions via max pooling.
5	Fully Connected Layer	`C.layers.Dense(units, activation)`	Defines a fully connected (dense) layer.

Syntax Explanation:

1. Define Input Variable

What is an Input Variable in CNNs?

Input variables define the structure of the input tensor for an image dataset, specifying its height, width, and number of channels.

Syntax:

`X = C.input_variable((32, 32, 3))`

Expanded Explanation:

- `C.input_variable((32, 32, 3))` creates an input tensor for images of size 32x32 with 3 color channels (RGB).
- Used in image classification, object detection, and medical imaging.
- Ensures that image data is properly formatted before entering the CNN.
- Supports different input shapes depending on the dataset, such as grayscale `(32, 32, 1)`.
- Helps the network learn spatial relationships by keeping structured input dimensions.

Example:
```
import cntk as C
X = C.input_variable((32, 32, 3))
print("Input Variable Shape:", X.shape)
```

Example Explanation:
- Confirms input shape, ensuring correct data formatting for CNNs.
- Ensures compatibility with convolutional layers.
- Verifies that the input size matches the expected dimensions of the dataset.

2. Convolutional Layer

What is a Convolutional Layer?
A convolutional layer applies small learnable filters to detect spatial patterns in input images.
Syntax:
```
conv_layer = C.layers.Convolution2D((3,3), 32,
activation=C.relu)(X)
```

Expanded Explanation:
- `C.layers.Convolution2D((3,3), 32,`
  `activation=C.relu)` defines a convolutional layer with a 3x3 kernel and 32 filters.
- Extracts meaningful spatial features like edges and textures.
- Uses ReLU activation to introduce non-linearity and prevent vanishing gradients.
- The number of filters can be adjusted based on network depth and complexity.
- Helps in hierarchical feature extraction, progressively learning abstract representations.

Example:
```
conv_layer = C.layers.Convolution2D((3,3), 32,
activation=C.relu)(X)
print("Convolutional Layer Output Shape:",
conv_layer.shape)
```

Example Explanation:
- Displays output shape after convolution, ensuring correct feature extraction.
- Verifies that the layer captures meaningful patterns from images.
- Helps check if the filter size and stride match the expected feature extraction requirements.

3. Apply ReLU Activation

What is ReLU?
ReLU (Rectified Linear Unit) is an activation function that sets negative values to zero while keeping positive values unchanged.
Syntax:
```
C.relu(x)
```

Expanded Explanation:
- `C.relu(x)` introduces non-linearity into the network, allowing it to learn complex patterns.
- Prevents the vanishing gradient problem by allowing gradients to flow through the network.
- Helps CNNs capture hierarchical feature representations in images.
- Reduces computation costs compared to sigmoid and tanh functions.
- Variants include Leaky ReLU (`C.leaky_relu(x, alpha=0.01)`) for improved training stability.

Example:
```
relu_output = C.relu(conv_layer)
print("ReLU Activation Applied")
```

Example Explanation:
- Ensures that negative values are set to zero.
- Helps enhance model training efficiency and performance.
- Prevents dead neurons by keeping a portion of the input active.

4. Max Pooling Layer

What is Max Pooling?

Max pooling is a downsampling technique that reduces the spatial dimensions of feature maps while retaining the most important features.

Syntax:

```
pooled_output = C.layers.MaxPooling((2,2),
strides=(2,2))(conv_layer)
```

Expanded Explanation:

- `C.layers.MaxPooling((2,2), strides=(2,2))` applies a 2x2 pooling operation with a stride of 2.
- Helps reduce computational complexity by decreasing the number of activations.
- Preserves the strongest features by selecting the maximum value in each pooling region.
- Prevents overfitting by making the model invariant to small spatial shifts.
- Alternative: `C.layers.AvgPooling()` which averages values instead of taking the maximum.

Example:

```
pooled_output = C.layers.MaxPooling((2,2),
strides=(2,2))(conv_layer)
print("Max Pooling Layer Output Shape:",
pooled_output.shape)
```

Example Explanation:

- Reduces feature map size while preserving key features.
- Helps CNNs learn more generalizable representations.
- Ensures spatial hierarchies are effectively captured.

5. Fully Connected Layer

What is a Fully Connected Layer?

A fully connected (dense) layer connects every neuron in the previous layer to every neuron in the next layer.

Syntax:
```
dense_output = C.layers.Dense(128,
activation=C.relu)(flattened_output)
```

Expanded Explanation:
- `C.layers.Dense(128, activation=C.relu)` creates a dense layer with 128 neurons and a ReLU activation function.
- Used for high-level feature abstraction after convolutional and pooling layers.
- Converts spatially reduced feature maps into final classification representations.
- Typically placed at the end of CNN architectures before softmax layers.
- Helps perform complex decision-making by processing extracted features.

Example:
```
flattened_output = C.reshape(pooled_output, (-1,))
dense_output = C.layers.Dense(128,
activation=C.relu)(flattened_output)
print("Fully Connected Layer Output Shape:",
dense_output.shape)
```

Example Explanation:
- Flattens pooled feature maps into a 1D vector for dense layers.
- Applies a fully connected layer for high-level feature interpretation.
- Ensures learned features contribute to final classification.

Real-Life Project: Building an Image Classifier with CNNs

Project Name: Image Classification Using Convolutional Neural Networks in CNTK

Project Overview: This project demonstrates how to build a CNN for classifying images into multiple categories using CNTK.

Project Goal:
- Implement a CNN for image classification.

- Train the model on a dataset of labeled images.
- Evaluate accuracy using a softmax classifier.

Code for This Project:

```python
import cntk as C
import numpy as np

def train_cnn_model():
    X = C.input_variable((32, 32, 3))
    Y = C.input_variable((10,))

    # Define CNN architecture
    conv1 = C.layers.Convolution2D((3,3), 32,
activation=C.relu)(X)
    pool1 = C.layers.MaxPooling((2,2),
strides=(2,2))(conv1)
    conv2 = C.layers.Convolution2D((3,3), 64,
activation=C.relu)(pool1)
    pool2 = C.layers.MaxPooling((2,2),
strides=(2,2))(conv2)

    # Flatten and fully connected layers
    flatten = C.reshape(pool2, (-1,))
    fc = C.layers.Dense(128,
activation=C.relu)(flatten)
    model = C.layers.Dense(10,
activation=C.softmax)(fc)

    # Define loss function and trainer
    loss = C.cross_entropy_with_softmax(model, Y)
    learner = C.adam_sgd(model.parameters,
C.learning_parameter_schedule(0.01))
    trainer = C.Trainer(model, (loss, None), [learner])

    # Generate dummy data
    data = np.random.rand(100, 32, 32,
3).astype(np.float32)
    labels = np.eye(10)[np.random.choice(10,
```

```python
100)].astype(np.float32)

    # Train model for 5 epochs
    for epoch in range(5):
        trainer.train_minibatch({X: data, Y: labels})
        print(f"Epoch {epoch+1}: Loss =",
trainer.previous_minibatch_loss_average)

    print("Training completed.")

train_cnn_model()
```

Expected Output:

```
Epoch 1: Loss = 2.3
Epoch 2: Loss = 1.8
...
Epoch 5: Loss = 0.9
Training completed.
```

Explanation:

- Uses convolutional and max-pooling layers to extract spatial features.
- Applies ReLU activation to enhance non-linearity.
- Trains using cross-entropy loss to optimize classification accuracy.

This project provides hands-on experience in implementing and training CNNs for image classification using CNTK.

Chapter 14: Configuring the Training Process in CNTK

This chapter explores how to configure the training process in CNTK, including defining loss functions, choosing optimization techniques, setting batch sizes, and tracking model performance. Proper training configuration is essential to ensure efficient and accurate deep learning model convergence.

Key Characteristics of Training in CNTK:

- **Loss Functions:** Measures the difference between predicted and actual outputs.
- **Optimizers:** Updates model parameters to minimize loss (e.g., Adam, SGD, RMSProp).
- **Batch Processing:** Efficiently processes multiple samples in a single training step.
- **Performance Metrics:** Tracks accuracy and loss over time to evaluate model performance.
- **Checkpointing:** Saves model states at intervals to prevent data loss during training.

Basic Rules for Configuring Training in CNTK:

- Select an appropriate loss function based on the problem type (classification, regression, etc.).
- Use optimizers like adam_sgd for adaptive learning or sgd for standard gradient descent.
- Tune batch sizes to balance training speed and model stability.
- Monitor validation loss to detect overfitting and adjust hyperparameters accordingly.
- Save model checkpoints periodically to resume training if interrupted.

Syntax Table:

SL NO	Function	Syntax/Example	Description
1	Define Loss Function	`C.cross_entrop y_with_softmax (pred, labels)`	Specifies the loss function for classification.
2	Choose Optimizer	`C.adam_sgd(mod el.parameters, lr_schedule)`	Selects an optimizer to update model weights.
3	Set Batch Size	`minibatch_size = 32`	Defines the number of samples per training step.
4	Track Performance	`trainer.previo us_minibatch_l oss_average`	Retrieves loss value after each step.
5	Save Checkpoint	`trainer.save_c heckpoint('mod el.ckpt')`	Saves model state for later resumption.

Syntax Explanation:

1. Define Loss Function

What is a Loss Function?
A loss function measures how well a model's predictions match the true labels, guiding optimization during training.

Syntax:
`loss = C.cross_entropy_with_softmax(pred, labels)`

Expanded Explanation:
- `C.cross_entropy_with_softmax(pred, labels)` computes the loss for multi-class classification tasks.
- Penalizes incorrect predictions and guides parameter updates.
- Ensures softmax normalization of output probabilities before computing cross-entropy.
- Common alternatives: `C.squared_error()` for regression and `C.binary_cross_entropy()` for binary classification.
- Helps fine-tune model predictions by minimizing classification errors.

- Essential for optimizing deep learning models using backpropagation.

Example:
```
import cntk as C
pred = C.input_variable((10,))
labels = C.input_variable((10,))
loss = C.cross_entropy_with_softmax(pred, labels)
print("Loss function defined.")
```

Example Explanation:
- Defines a loss function for classification.
- Ensures correct label matching in supervised learning tasks.
- Helps models learn and improve accuracy over training epochs.

2. Choose Optimizer

What is an Optimizer?
An optimizer adjusts model weights to minimize the loss function during training.
Syntax:
```
learner = C.adam_sgd(model.parameters,
C.learning_parameter_schedule(0.01))
```
Expanded Explanation:
- `C.adam_sgd(model.parameters,`
  `C.learning_parameter_schedule(0.01))` applies Adam optimization with a learning rate of `0.01`.
- Adam combines momentum and adaptive learning rates for faster convergence.
- Alternative optimizers: `C.sgd()` for standard gradient descent and `C.momentum_sgd()` for accelerated training.
- Helps prevent model divergence by dynamically adjusting learning rates.
- Particularly effective for training deep neural networks.

Example:
```
learner = C.adam_sgd(model.parameters,
C.learning_parameter_schedule(0.01))
print("Optimizer initialized.")
```

Example Explanation:
- Defines an adaptive optimizer to update model weights efficiently.
- Ensures faster and stable convergence in deep learning models.

3. Set Batch Size

What is a Batch Size?
Batch size determines the number of samples processed before updating model parameters.
Syntax:
```
minibatch_size = 32
```

Expanded Explanation:
- `minibatch_size = 32` sets batch size to 32 samples per training iteration.
- Helps balance training efficiency and memory usage.
- Smaller batch sizes provide frequent updates but may increase noise in gradients.
- Larger batch sizes offer smoother convergence but require more memory.
- Essential for tuning training stability and performance.

Example:
```
minibatch_size = 32
print("Batch size set to:", minibatch_size)
```

Example Explanation:
- Confirms batch size for training iterations.
- Ensures an optimal balance between accuracy and computational efficiency.

4. Track Performance

What is Performance Tracking?
Tracking loss and accuracy helps evaluate model training progress.

Syntax:
```
trainer.previous_minibatch_loss_average
```

Expanded Explanation:
- `trainer.previous_minibatch_loss_average` retrieves the average loss from the last training step.
- Helps monitor training stability and convergence.
- Can be logged over epochs to visualize improvement trends.
- Essential for detecting overfitting and adjusting hyperparameters accordingly.

Example:
```
print("Latest training loss:",
trainer.previous_minibatch_loss_average)
```

Example Explanation:
- Displays the latest loss value for real-time monitoring.
- Helps track model improvements across multiple epochs.

5. Save Checkpoint

What is a Checkpoint?
A checkpoint saves model parameters, allowing training to resume from the last saved state if interrupted.

Syntax:
```
trainer.save_checkpoint('model.ckpt')
```

Expanded Explanation:
- `trainer.save_checkpoint('model.ckpt')` stores the model weights and optimizer state.
- Prevents data loss in case of unexpected interruptions.
- Enables model resumption without starting from scratch.
- Useful for training large models over extended periods.

Example:
```
trainer.save_checkpoint('model_epoch1.ckpt')
print("Checkpoint saved.")
```

Example Explanation:
- Saves the model after each epoch to maintain progress.
- Ensures efficient training resumption if halted unexpectedly.

Real-Life Project: Configuring Training for an Image Classifier

Project Name: Training an Image Classifier with Optimized Parameters

Project Overview: This project demonstrates how to configure the training process for a CNN-based image classification model using CNTK.

Project Goal:

- Define an appropriate loss function for classification.
- Select an optimizer and configure batch size for efficient training.
- Track model performance and save training checkpoints.

Code for This Project:

```
import cntk as C
import numpy as np

def train_image_classifier():
    X = C.input_variable((32, 32, 3))
    Y = C.input_variable((10,))

    # Define CNN model
    conv1 = C.layers.Convolution2D((3,3), 32,
activation=C.relu)(X)
    pool1 = C.layers.MaxPooling((2,2),
strides=(2,2))(conv1)
    conv2 = C.layers.Convolution2D((3,3), 64,
activation=C.relu)(pool1)
    pool2 = C.layers.MaxPooling((2,2),
strides=(2,2))(conv2)

    flatten = C.reshape(pool2, (-1,))
    fc = C.layers.Dense(128,
activation=C.relu)(flatten)
    model = C.layers.Dense(10,
activation=C.softmax)(fc)

    # Define loss function and optimizer
    loss = C.cross_entropy_with_softmax(model, Y)
```

```python
    learner = C.adam_sgd(model.parameters,
C.learning_parameter_schedule(0.01))
    trainer = C.Trainer(model, (loss, None), [learner])

    # Generate dummy data
    data = np.random.rand(100, 32, 32,
3).astype(np.float32)
    labels = np.eye(10)[np.random.choice(10,
100)].astype(np.float32)
    minibatch_size = 32

    # Train model for 5 epochs with batch processing
    for epoch in range(5):
        for i in range(0, len(data), minibatch_size):
            batch_data = data[i:i+minibatch_size]
            batch_labels = labels[i:i+minibatch_size]
            trainer.train_minibatch({X: batch_data, Y:
batch_labels})
        print(f"Epoch {epoch+1}: Loss =",
trainer.previous_minibatch_loss_average)

trainer.save_checkpoint(f'model_epoch{epoch+1}.ckpt')
    print("Training completed.")
train_image_classifier()
```

Expected Output:
```
Epoch 1: Loss = 2.2
Epoch 2: Loss = 1.7
...
Epoch 5: Loss = 0.8
Training completed.
```
Explanation:
- Configures loss function and optimizer for classification.
- Uses mini-batch processing for efficient learning.
- Saves model checkpoints at each epoch to track progress.

This project provides hands-on experience in optimizing and configuring training workflows in CNTK.

Chapter 15: Working with CNTK's Learners for Optimization

This chapter explores how to use CNTK's Learners for optimizing deep learning models. Learners define the optimization algorithms that adjust model parameters to minimize loss and improve performance. CNTK provides several built-in learners like Stochastic Gradient Descent (SGD), Adam, RMSProp, and Momentum SGD, each suited for different training scenarios. Understanding and configuring these learners is essential for efficient model convergence.

Key Characteristics of CNTK's Learners:

- **Gradient-Based Optimization:** Learners update model weights using computed gradients.
- **Adaptive Learning Rates:** Some learners dynamically adjust learning rates to improve convergence.
- **Momentum-Based Updates:** Helps models overcome local minima and improve stability.
- **Regularization Support:** Includes L1 and L2 regularization for better generalization.
- **Scalability:** Optimized for large datasets and GPU acceleration.

Basic Rules for Using Learners in CNTK:

- Choose `sgd` for simple gradient descent updates.
- Use `adam_sgd` for adaptive learning rate optimization.
- Apply `momentum_sgd` to accelerate convergence using past gradients.
- Utilize `rmsprop` for training models with non-stationary objectives.
- Regularize model weights using L2 regularization (`l2_regularization_weight`).

Syntax Table:

SL NO	Function	Syntax/Example	Description
1	Stochastic Gradient Descent (SGD)	`C.sgd(model.parameters, lr_schedule)`	Implements standard gradient descent.
2	Adam Optimizer	`C.adam_sgd(model.parameters, lr_schedule)`	Uses adaptive learning rates for optimization.
3	Momentum SGD	`C.momentum_sgd(model.parameters, lr_schedule, momentum)`	Uses momentum to accelerate learning.
4	RMSProp Optimizer	`C.rmsprop(model.parameters, lr_schedule)`	Optimizes models with adaptive learning rates.
5	Apply L2 Regularizatio n	`C.adam_sgd(model.parameters, lr_schedule, l2_regularization_weight=0.01)`	Regularizes model weights.

Syntax Explanation:

1. Stochastic Gradient Descent (SGD)

What is SGD?
SGD is the most basic optimization algorithm that updates weights based on individual gradients computed from training data.
Syntax:
```
learner = C.sgd(model.parameters,
C.learning_parameter_schedule(0.01))
```

Expanded Explanation:
- `C.sgd(model.parameters, C.learning_parameter_schedule(0.01))` applies basic gradient descent with a learning rate of `0.01`.

- Updates weights using gradients computed from mini-batches.
- Prone to slow convergence, but effective in simple models.
- Best suited for convex optimization problems.
- Can be combined with momentum (`C.momentum_sgd`) to improve stability and speed.
- Learning rate schedules can be applied to dynamically adjust learning rates over epochs.

Example:
```
learner = C.sgd(model.parameters,
C.learning_parameter_schedule(0.01))
print("SGD optimizer initialized.")
```

Example Explanation:
- Defines an SGD optimizer with a fixed learning rate.
- Updates model weights based on computed gradients.
- Helps track learning rate adjustments over time.

2. Adam Optimizer

What is Adam?
Adam is an adaptive learning rate optimization algorithm that adjusts learning rates per parameter.

Syntax:
```
learner = C.adam_sgd(model.parameters,
C.learning_parameter_schedule(0.01))
```

Expanded Explanation:
- `C.adam_sgd(model.parameters, C.learning_parameter_schedule(0.01))` applies the Adam optimization algorithm with an initial learning rate of `0.01`.
- Combines the advantages of `sgd` and `rmsprop` to balance adaptive learning and stability.
- Efficient for large datasets and non-stationary objectives.
- Reduces sensitivity to initial learning rate selection.
- Uses moving averages of gradients and squared gradients to scale updates dynamically.

Example:
```
learner = C.adam_sgd(model.parameters,
C.learning_parameter_schedule(0.01))
print("Adam optimizer initialized.")
```

Example Explanation:
- Implements Adam for faster convergence.
- Automatically adjusts learning rates based on gradient history.

3. Momentum SGD

What is Momentum SGD?
Momentum-based optimization accelerates gradient descent by maintaining a moving average of past gradients.
Syntax:
```
learner = C.momentum_sgd(model.parameters,
C.learning_parameter_schedule(0.01), momentum=0.9)
```

Expanded Explanation:
- Uses momentum (momentum=0.9) to prevent oscillations and accelerate convergence.
- Helps models overcome shallow local minima.
- Can be combined with adaptive learning rate schedules for improved training efficiency.
- Reduces training noise by smoothing parameter updates.

Example:
```
learner = C.momentum_sgd(model.parameters,
C.learning_parameter_schedule(0.01), momentum=0.9)
print("Momentum SGD optimizer initialized.")
```

Example Explanation:
- Applies momentum to stabilize gradient updates.
- Reduces training time by propagating useful past gradient information.

4. RMSProp Optimizer

What is RMSProp?
RMSProp is an adaptive optimization algorithm that normalizes gradients by their magnitude.
Syntax:
```
learner = C.rmsprop(model.parameters,
C.learning_parameter_schedule(0.01))
```

Expanded Explanation:
- `C.rmsprop(model.parameters,`
  `C.learning_parameter_schedule(0.01))` uses an adaptive learning rate for each parameter.
- Normalizes updates to prevent rapid swings in parameter updates.
- Especially useful for models with non-stationary loss landscapes.
- Can improve convergence on deep networks where SGD struggles.

Example:
```
learner = C.rmsprop(model.parameters,
C.learning_parameter_schedule(0.01))
print("RMSProp optimizer initialized.")
```

Example Explanation:
- Ensures stable learning rates.
- Reduces drastic weight updates, maintaining smoother convergence.

5. Apply L2 Regularization

What is L2 Regularization?
L2 regularization penalizes large weights, preventing overfitting.
Syntax:
```
learner = C.adam_sgd(model.parameters,
C.learning_parameter_schedule(0.01),
l2_regularization_weight=0.01)
```

Expanded Explanation:

- Adds a regularization term (l2_regularization_weight=0.01) to limit large parameter values.
- Helps improve model generalization and prevents overfitting.
- Often combined with dropout layers for additional regularization.
- Ensures weight magnitudes stay within reasonable limits.

Example:

```
learner = C.adam_sgd(model.parameters,
C.learning_parameter_schedule(0.01),
l2_regularization_weight=0.01)
print("L2 Regularization applied to Adam optimizer.")
```

Example Explanation:

- Demonstrates how to add L2 regularization to an optimizer.
- Helps reduce overfitting by penalizing large weight values.

Real-Life Project: Comparing Learners in CNTK

Project Name: Evaluating Different Optimization Algorithms in CNTK

Project Overview: This project demonstrates how to compare different learners (SGD, Adam, and Momentum SGD) for optimizing a neural network.

Project Goal:

- Train a simple neural network using different learners.
- Evaluate and compare performance based on loss reduction.
- Choose the best learner for the given dataset.

Code for This Project:

```
import cntk as C
import numpy as np

def train_model_with_learner(learner_type):
    X = C.input_variable((100,))
    Y = C.input_variable((10,))

    model = C.layers.Dense(64, activation=C.relu)(X)
```

```python
    model = C.layers.Dense(10,
activation=C.softmax)(model)

    loss = C.cross_entropy_with_softmax(model, Y)

    if learner_type == "sgd":
        learner = C.sgd(model.parameters,
C.learning_parameter_schedule(0.01))
    elif learner_type == "adam":
        learner = C.adam_sgd(model.parameters,
C.learning_parameter_schedule(0.01))
    elif learner_type == "momentum":
        learner = C.momentum_sgd(model.parameters,
C.learning_parameter_schedule(0.01), momentum=0.9)

    trainer = C.Trainer(model, (loss, None), [learner])

    data = np.random.rand(100, 100).astype(np.float32)
    labels = np.eye(10)[np.random.choice(10,
100)].astype(np.float32)

    for epoch in range(5):
        trainer.train_minibatch({X: data, Y: labels})
        print(f"Epoch {epoch+1} ({learner_type}): Loss
=", trainer.previous_minibatch_loss_average)

    print(f"Training completed using {learner_type}.")

train_model_with_learner("sgd")
train_model_with_learner("adam")
train_model_with_learner("momentum")
```

Expected Output:

```
Epoch 1 (sgd): Loss = 2.3
Epoch 2 (sgd): Loss = 1.9
...
Epoch 5 (sgd): Loss = 1.2
```

```
Training completed using sgd.
Epoch 1 (adam): Loss = 2.1
Epoch 2 (adam): Loss = 1.5
...
Epoch 5 (adam): Loss = 0.8
Training completed using adam.
Epoch 1 (momentum): Loss = 2.2
Epoch 2 (momentum): Loss = 1.6
...
Epoch 5 (momentum): Loss = 0.9
Training completed using momentum.
```

Explanation:

- Trains the same model with different learners and compares loss reduction.
- Evaluates the effectiveness of each learner for optimization.
- Helps in selecting the best optimization strategy for a given task.

This project provides practical insights into using and tuning different learners for training deep learning models in CNTK.

Chapter 16: Training with Mini-Batches and Data Streams in CNTK

This chapter explores how to train deep learning models efficiently using mini-batches and data streams in CNTK. Mini-batch training improves performance by processing small subsets of data at a time, rather than the entire dataset. Data streams in CNTK enable handling large datasets efficiently by loading data in chunks instead of keeping everything in memory.

Key Characteristics of Mini-Batches and Data Streams in CNTK:

- **Efficient Memory Utilization:** Processes smaller data batches, reducing memory overhead.
- **Faster Training:** Allows parallelism and optimization when using GPUs.
- **Generalization:** Improves model generalization by updating weights more frequently.
- **Data Streaming:** Loads large datasets dynamically, avoiding memory overload.
- **Scalability:** Suitable for handling massive datasets in real-world applications.

Basic Rules for Training with Mini-Batches and Data Streams:

- Define a `MinibatchSource` to load data dynamically.
- Set an appropriate batch size to balance computation speed and accuracy.
- Use `next_minibatch()` to fetch data iteratively during training.
- Shuffle data to prevent learning order-dependent patterns.
- Monitor validation loss to ensure stable learning.

Syntax Table:

SL NO	Function	Syntax/Example	Description
1	Define Mini-Batch Source	`C.io.MinibatchSource(data_path, ...)`	Loads dataset in mini-batches dynamically.
2	Set Mini-Batch Size	`minibatch_size = 32`	Defines number of samples per training iteration.
3	Fetch Next Mini-Batch	`data = minibatch_source.next_minibatch(32)`	Retrieves the next batch of training data.
4	Shuffle Data	`randomize=True` in `MinibatchSource`	Enables shuffling for better generalization.
5	Track Mini-Batch Loss	`trainer.previous_minibatch_loss_average`	Monitors loss value during mini-batch training.

Syntax Explanation:

1. Define Mini-Batch Source

What is a Mini-Batch Source?
A `MinibatchSource` loads data dynamically, allowing models to train on large datasets without loading everything into memory.
Syntax:
```
minibatch_source =
C.io.MinibatchSource(C.io.CTFDeserializer("data.ctf",
...))
```
Expanded Explanation:
- `C.io.MinibatchSource()` initializes a data loader that streams data in chunks.
- Supports various file formats like CTF, CSV, and `ImageDeserializer`.
- Prevents memory overload by loading data only when needed.

- Essential for training on large datasets such as image or text corpora.
- Enhances scalability by allowing parallel data loading across multiple GPUs.

Example:

```
import cntk as C
minibatch_source =
C.io.MinibatchSource(C.io.CTFDeserializer("data.ctf",
...))
print("Mini-Batch Source initialized.")
```

Example Explanation:
- Creates a mini-batch data loader.
- Ensures efficient data streaming for large-scale training.
- Allows users to dynamically adjust the number of mini-batches processed.

2. Set Mini-Batch Size

What is a Mini-Batch Size?
Mini-batch size determines how many training samples are processed at once before updating model weights.

Syntax:

```
minibatch_size = 32
```

Expanded Explanation:
- `minibatch_size = 32` processes 32 samples per training iteration.
- Affects training stability, convergence speed, and memory consumption.
- Smaller batch sizes provide more frequent weight updates but can introduce noise.
- Larger batch sizes improve stability but require more memory.
- Adaptive mini-batch sizing can be used to optimize GPU utilization.

Example:
```
minibatch_size = 32
print("Mini-Batch Size Set To:", minibatch_size)
```

Example Explanation:
- Ensures mini-batch size is correctly defined.
- Helps maintain a balance between computational efficiency and accuracy.
- Prevents memory overflow when training on large datasets.

3. Fetch Next Mini-Batch

What is Next Mini-Batch?
This function retrieves the next batch of training data from the data stream.
Syntax:
```
data = minibatch_source.next_minibatch(32)
```

Expanded Explanation:
- `minibatch_source.next_minibatch(32)` fetches a new batch of 32 samples.
- Dynamically loads data during training without preloading the entire dataset.
- Prevents memory constraints by efficiently handling large-scale data.
- Works in combination with `MinibatchSource` to allow sequential processing of data.
- Supports various data augmentation techniques to improve model generalization.

Example:
```
data = minibatch_source.next_minibatch(32)
print("Fetched Mini-Batch Data.")
```

Example Explanation:
- Fetches new data samples during training.
- Ensures smooth and memory-efficient data loading.
- Helps maintain training consistency over multiple epochs.

4. Shuffle Data

What is Data Shuffling?
Shuffling data ensures that models learn generalized patterns rather than memorizing order-dependent relationships.

Syntax:
```
minibatch_source =
C.io.MinibatchSource(C.io.CTFDeserializer("data.ctf",
...), randomize=True)
```

Expanded Explanation:
- `randomize=True` enables data shuffling within the mini-batch loader.
- Prevents overfitting by ensuring diverse sample exposure to the model.
- Helps prevent convergence issues caused by repetitive training order.
- Ensures each epoch has a different order of training samples, improving robustness.
- Often combined with data augmentation techniques for enhanced learning.

Example:
```
minibatch_source =
C.io.MinibatchSource(C.io.CTFDeserializer("data.ctf",
...), randomize=True)
print("Data Shuffling Enabled.")
```

Example Explanation:
- Randomizes dataset order for each training epoch.
- Improves generalization performance across unseen data.
- Ensures equal representation of all classes in classification tasks.

5. Track Mini-Batch Loss

What is Mini-Batch Loss Tracking?
Tracking mini-batch loss provides insights into model performance across training iterations.
Syntax:
```
loss = trainer.previous_minibatch_loss_average
```

Expanded Explanation:
- Retrieves the average loss computed over the last mini-batch.
- Helps monitor convergence trends and detect potential overfitting.
- Can be logged over multiple epochs to analyze training stability.
- Assists in adjusting learning rates dynamically for better optimization.
- Provides real-time feedback during training, enabling proactive model tuning.

Example:
```
print("Current Mini-Batch Loss:",
trainer.previous_minibatch_loss_average)
```

Example Explanation:
- Displays the latest computed mini-batch loss value.
- Helps validate whether the model is learning efficiently.
- Enables tuning of hyperparameters based on real-time loss evaluation.

Real-Life Project: Training an Image Classifier with Mini-Batches

Project Name: Image Classification using Mini-Batches in CNTK
Project Overview: This project demonstrates how to train a CNN model using mini-batches and data streams to efficiently handle large-scale image datasets.
Project Goal:
- Implement mini-batch processing to improve training

efficiency.
- Load image data dynamically using CNTK's `MinibatchSource`.
- Track mini-batch loss and accuracy to optimize training.

Code for This Project:

```python
import cntk as C
import numpy as np

def train_cnn_model():
    X = C.input_variable((32, 32, 3))
    Y = C.input_variable((10,))

    # Define CNN architecture
    conv1 = C.layers.Convolution2D((3,3), 32,
activation=C.relu)(X)
    pool1 = C.layers.MaxPooling((2,2),
strides=(2,2))(conv1)
    conv2 = C.layers.Convolution2D((3,3), 64,
activation=C.relu)(pool1)
    pool2 = C.layers.MaxPooling((2,2),
strides=(2,2))(conv2)

    flatten = C.reshape(pool2, (-1,))
    fc = C.layers.Dense(128,
activation=C.relu)(flatten)
    model = C.layers.Dense(10,
activation=C.softmax)(fc)

    # Define loss function and optimizer
    loss = C.cross_entropy_with_softmax(model, Y)
    learner = C.adam_sgd(model.parameters,
C.learning_parameter_schedule(0.01))
    trainer = C.Trainer(model, (loss, None), [learner])

    # Load dataset using MinibatchSource
    minibatch_source =
```

```
C.io.MinibatchSource(C.io.CTFDeserializer("data.ctf",
...))
    minibatch_size = 32

    # Train model for 5 epochs with mini-batch
processing
    for epoch in range(5):
        for _ in range(100):   # Simulating 100 mini-
batches per epoch
            data =
minibatch_source.next_minibatch(minibatch_size)
            trainer.train_minibatch({X:
data["features"], Y: data["labels"]})
        print(f"Epoch {epoch+1}: Loss =",
trainer.previous_minibatch_loss_average)

    print("Training completed.")

train_cnn_model()
```

Expected Output:

```
Epoch 1: Loss = 2.3
Epoch 2: Loss = 1.8
...
Epoch 5: Loss = 0.9
Training completed.
```

Explanation:
- Implements mini-batch processing to improve memory efficiency.
- Loads image data dynamically using MinibatchSource.
- Tracks training loss over multiple mini-batches for optimization.

This project provides hands-on experience in optimizing training workflows using mini-batches and data streams in CNTK.

Chapter 17: Early Stopping and Model Checkpoints in CNTK

This chapter explores early stopping and model checkpoints in CNTK. Early stopping prevents overfitting by halting training when validation loss stops improving. Model checkpoints enable saving model states at intervals to resume training if interrupted or to retain the best-performing model.

Key Characteristics of Early Stopping and Checkpoints in CNTK:

- **Overfitting Prevention:** Stops training when validation performance degrades.
- **Efficiency:** Reduces unnecessary training time while maintaining performance.
- **Model Recovery:** Saves model checkpoints periodically for resumption.
- **Performance Monitoring:** Tracks validation loss and accuracy over epochs.
- **Best Model Selection:** Allows saving the best model state for deployment.

Basic Rules for Early Stopping and Model Checkpoints:

- Monitor validation loss using `trainer.previous_minibatch_loss_average`.
- Define a patience parameter to allow small fluctuations before stopping.
- Save checkpoints periodically using `trainer.save_checkpoint("model.ckpt")`.
- Resume training from a checkpoint using `trainer.restore_from_checkpoint("model.ckpt")`.
- Use early stopping when validation loss does not improve for several epochs.

Syntax Table:

SL NO	Function	Syntax/Example	Description
1	Track Validation Loss	`trainer.previous_minibatch_loss_average`	Monitors loss to detect overfitting.
2	Define Early Stopping	Custom condition based on validation loss	Stops training when loss stops improving.
3	Save Model Checkpoint	`trainer.save_checkpoint('model.ckpt')`	Saves the current model state.
4	Restore Model from Checkpoint	`trainer.restore_from_checkpoint('model.ckpt')`	Resumes training from a checkpoint.
5	Store Best Model	Conditional checkpoint saving	Saves the model with the lowest validation loss.

Syntax Explanation:

1. Track Validation Loss

What is Validation Loss Tracking?
Validation loss is used to assess model generalization performance and detect overfitting.
Syntax:
`val_loss = trainer.previous_minibatch_loss_average`

Expanded Explanation:
- Retrieves the loss computed on the validation set.
- Helps track model performance over multiple epochs.
- Used as a metric for early stopping and best model selection.
- Can be logged and visualized for trend analysis.
- Prevents unnecessary training when no further improvements occur.
- Assists in dynamic learning rate adjustments if required.

Example:
```
print("Validation Loss:",
trainer.previous_minibatch_loss_average)
```

Example Explanation:
- Displays the latest validation loss value.
- Helps in deciding whether to continue training or stop.
- Provides insights into model stability and convergence trends.

2. Define Early Stopping

What is Early Stopping?
Early stopping prevents overfitting by stopping training when validation loss stops improving for a set number of epochs.
Syntax:
```
if epochs_without_improvement >= patience:
    print("Early stopping triggered.")
    break
```
Expanded Explanation:
- Monitors the number of epochs without improvement in validation loss.
- Stops training if loss does not decrease for a specified patience value.
- Prevents unnecessary computations and saves time.
- Helps select an optimal stopping point while maintaining model accuracy.

Example:
```
if epochs_without_improvement >= 3:
    print("Early stopping triggered.")
    break
```
Example Explanation:
- Stops training if no improvement is observed over 3 consecutive epochs.
- Prevents unnecessary overfitting by ensuring training halts at the right time.
- Allows better resource utilization and optimized training duration.

3. Save Model Checkpoint

What is a Model Checkpoint?
Model checkpoints save a model's parameters at specific intervals to allow recovery in case of failures.
Syntax:
```
trainer.save_checkpoint("model.ckpt")
```

Expanded Explanation:
- Saves the model weights and optimizer state.
- Prevents loss of progress in case of system crashes.
- Enables model evaluation at different training stages.
- Useful for experimenting with hyperparameter tuning.

Example:
```
trainer.save_checkpoint("best_model.ckpt")
print("Model checkpoint saved.")
```

Example Explanation:
- Stores the best-performing model checkpoint.
- Ensures recovery from interruptions and allows reproducibility.
- Enables training resumption without loss of progress.

4. Restore Model from Checkpoint

What is Restoring from a Checkpoint?
Restoring a model from a checkpoint allows resuming training from where it last stopped.
Syntax:
```
trainer.restore_from_checkpoint("model.ckpt")
```

Expanded Explanation:
- Loads the saved model state for further training.
- Prevents the need to restart training from scratch.
- Useful for running training in multiple sessions.
- Enables comparative performance evaluation across different saved states.

Example:
```
trainer.restore_from_checkpoint("best_model.ckpt")
print("Checkpoint restored. Training resumed.")
```

Example Explanation:
- Resumes training from the best saved state.
- Ensures continuity in model optimization and performance.
- Helps recover from interruptions without re-training from scratch.

5. Store Best Model

What is Best Model Storage?
Storing the best model ensures that the best-performing parameters are retained for final deployment.

Syntax:
```
if val_loss < best_loss:
    best_loss = val_loss
    trainer.save_checkpoint("best_model.ckpt")
```

Expanded Explanation:
- Compares the current validation loss with the previous best loss.
- Saves the model only if an improvement is detected.
- Ensures deployment-ready models are stored with optimal weights.
- Avoids unnecessary checkpoint storage for suboptimal models.

Example:
```
if val_loss < best_loss:
    best_loss = val_loss
    trainer.save_checkpoint("best_model.ckpt")
    print("New best model saved.")
```

Example Explanation:
- Saves the model checkpoint only if it achieves a new lowest validation loss.
- Ensures that only the best version of the model is retained.
- Avoids redundant storage of multiple similar checkpoints.

Real-Life Project: Implementing Early Stopping and Checkpoints in a CNN Model

Project Name: Early Stopping and Model Checkpoints for Image Classification

Project Overview: This project demonstrates how to implement early stopping and model checkpoints to optimize CNN training in CNTK.

Project Goal:

- Implement early stopping to prevent overfitting.
- Save model checkpoints at regular intervals.
- Restore the best-performing model for final evaluation.

Code for This Project:

```python
import cntk as C
import numpy as np

def train_cnn_with_early_stopping():
    X = C.input_variable((32, 32, 3))
    Y = C.input_variable((10,))

    # Define CNN model
    conv1 = C.layers.Convolution2D((3,3), 32,
activation=C.relu)(X)
    pool1 = C.layers.MaxPooling((2,2),
strides=(2,2))(conv1)
    conv2 = C.layers.Convolution2D((3,3), 64,
activation=C.relu)(pool1)
    pool2 = C.layers.MaxPooling((2,2),
strides=(2,2))(conv2)

    flatten = C.reshape(pool2, (-1,))
    fc = C.layers.Dense(128,
activation=C.relu)(flatten)
    model = C.layers.Dense(10,
activation=C.softmax)(fc)

    # Define loss function and optimizer
    loss = C.cross_entropy_with_softmax(model, Y)
```

```
    learner = C.adam_sgd(model.parameters,
C.learning_parameter_schedule(0.01))
    trainer = C.Trainer(model, (loss, None), [learner])

    # Training parameters
    minibatch_size = 32
    patience = 3  # Early stopping patience
    best_loss = float("inf")
    epochs_without_improvement = 0

    # Dummy training data
    data = np.random.rand(100, 32, 32,
3).astype(np.float32)
    labels = np.eye(10)[np.random.choice(10,
100)].astype(np.float32)

    # Train model with early stopping
    for epoch in range(20):  # Maximum 20 epochs
        for i in range(0, len(data), minibatch_size):
            batch_data = data[i:i+minibatch_size]
            batch_labels = labels[i:i+minibatch_size]
            trainer.train_minibatch({X: batch_data, Y:
batch_labels})

        val_loss =
trainer.previous_minibatch_loss_average
        print(f"Epoch {epoch+1}: Validation Loss =",
val_loss)

        # Check for early stopping
        if val_loss < best_loss:
            best_loss = val_loss
            epochs_without_improvement = 0
            trainer.save_checkpoint("best_model.ckpt")
            print("Checkpoint saved: Best model
updated.")
        else:
```

```
            epochs_without_improvement += 1
            if epochs_without_improvement >= patience:
                print("Early stopping triggered.")
                break

    print("Training completed.")

train_cnn_with_early_stopping()
```

Expected Output:

```
Epoch 1: Validation Loss = 2.3
Epoch 2: Validation Loss = 1.9
Checkpoint saved: Best model updated.
Epoch 3: Validation Loss = 1.6
Checkpoint saved: Best model updated.
...
Epoch 7: Validation Loss = 1.2
Checkpoint saved: Best model updated.
Epoch 10: Validation Loss = 1.2
Epoch 11: Validation Loss = 1.2
Epoch 12: Validation Loss = 1.2
Early stopping triggered.
Training completed.
```

Explanation:

- Implements early stopping by tracking validation loss and stopping after 3 epochs of no improvement.
- Saves checkpoints when validation loss improves.
- Ensures the best-performing model is retained for final evaluation.

This project provides practical experience in integrating early stopping and model checkpointing for optimized deep learning training in CNTK.

Chapter 18: Evaluating and Fine-Tuning Models in CNTK

This chapter explores how to evaluate and fine-tune trained models in CNTK. Model evaluation involves measuring accuracy, precision, recall, and loss on test datasets, while fine-tuning involves retraining models with adjusted hyperparameters, additional data, or modified architectures to improve performance.

Key Characteristics of Model Evaluation and Fine-Tuning in CNTK:

- **Performance Metrics:** Measures model effectiveness using accuracy, precision, recall, and loss.
- **Test Dataset Evaluation:** Runs trained models on unseen data to assess generalization.
- **Hyperparameter Adjustment:** Refines learning rates, batch sizes, and optimizers for improved learning.
- **Transfer Learning:** Reuses trained layers from pre-trained models for related tasks.
- **Error Analysis:** Identifies misclassified examples to refine model behavior.

Basic Rules for Evaluating and Fine-Tuning Models:

- Use a separate test dataset for final model evaluation.
- Compute performance metrics such as accuracy, precision, recall, and F1-score.
- Fine-tune models by adjusting learning rates or freezing certain layers.
- Use transfer learning for faster convergence on related tasks.
- Perform error analysis to refine the dataset and model training process.

Syntax Table:

SL NO	Function	Syntax/Example	Description
1	Evaluate Model Accuracy	`C.classification_error(predictions, labels)`	Computes classification accuracy on test data.
2	Compute Loss on Test Set	`C.cross_entropy_with_softmax(predictions, labels)`	Evaluates final model loss.
3	Fine-Tune Learning Rate	`C.learning_parameter_schedule(0.001)`	Adjusts the learning rate for better convergence.
4	Freeze Layers for Transfer Learning	`layer.freeze()`	Prevents selected layers from updating.
5	Identify Misclassified Samples	`np.where(predictions != labels)`	Helps analyze and refine model performance.

Syntax Explanation:

1. Evaluate Model Accuracy

What is Model Accuracy Evaluation?
Accuracy measures the percentage of correctly classified samples in a test dataset.
Syntax:
```
accuracy = C.classification_error(predictions, labels)
```

Expanded Explanation:
- Computes the fraction of misclassified examples.
- Used to compare different models and evaluate generalization performance.
- Can be used during training validation or final test evaluation.
- Lower classification error indicates a more accurate model.

- Can be combined with precision and recall for a deeper understanding of model performance.
- Helps in identifying possible class imbalance issues.

Example:
```
print("Model Accuracy:", 1 -
C.classification_error(predictions, labels).eval())
```

Example Explanation:
- Computes and prints the final model accuracy.
- Helps compare models trained with different hyperparameters.
- Provides an essential benchmark for evaluating fine-tuning improvements.

2. Compute Loss on Test Set
What is Loss Evaluation?
Loss function measures the difference between predicted and actual values, helping optimize models.

Syntax:
```
test_loss = C.cross_entropy_with_softmax(predictions,
labels)
```

Expanded Explanation:
- Computes how well the model predictions match actual labels.
- Lower loss values indicate better predictive performance.
- Useful for tracking training and validation progress over epochs.
- Helps in deciding when to stop training or adjust learning rates.
- Can be combined with early stopping for better generalization.

Example:
```
print("Test Loss:", test_loss.eval())
```
Example Explanation:
- Displays final test set loss after model training.
- Helps in diagnosing underfitting or overfitting issues.
- Can be monitored alongside accuracy to evaluate model improvements.

3. Fine-Tune Learning Rate

What is Learning Rate Fine-Tuning?
Adjusting the learning rate can significantly impact model convergence and accuracy.
Syntax:
```
learning_rate = C.learning_parameter_schedule(0.001)
```

Expanded Explanation:
- Lower learning rates help models fine-tune weights gradually.
- Higher learning rates can accelerate training but risk overshooting minima.
- Useful when fine-tuning pre-trained models on a new dataset.
- Can be adapted dynamically during training for better optimization.
- Helps achieve better generalization in transfer learning scenarios.

Example:
```
learner = C.adam_sgd(model.parameters,
C.learning_parameter_schedule(0.001))
print("Learning rate set for fine-tuning.")
```

Example Explanation:
- Configures an adaptive optimizer with a fine-tuned learning rate.
- Helps models adjust to new data distributions more effectively.
- Prevents drastic parameter updates that might destabilize training.

4. Freeze Layers for Transfer Learning

What is Freezing Layers in Transfer Learning?
Freezing layers helps retain pre-trained knowledge while fine-tuning higher layers for new tasks.

Syntax:
```
layer.freeze()
```

Expanded Explanation:
- Prevents earlier layers from updating, preserving learned features.
- Only final layers are trained for better generalization.
- Reduces computational cost and training time.
- Ideal for leveraging existing deep learning models for related tasks.
- Commonly used in image classification and NLP applications.

Example:
```
for layer in pretrained_model.layers[:-2]:
    layer.freeze()
print("Lower layers frozen for transfer learning.")
```

Example Explanation:
- Ensures the backbone layers of the model remain unchanged.
- Allows new layers to specialize in the new task efficiently.
- Speeds up fine-tuning by focusing updates only on higher layers.

5. Identify Misclassified Samples

What is Error Analysis?
Misclassified samples provide insight into dataset quality and model weaknesses.

Syntax:
```
misclassified = np.where(predictions != labels)
```

Expanded Explanation:
- Identifies incorrectly predicted labels.
- Useful for detecting class imbalances or annotation errors.
- Helps in designing better feature extraction or data augmentation strategies.
- Provides a roadmap for further improvements and refinements.

- Can be visualized to better understand model decision-making.

Example:
```
print("Misclassified Indices:", np.where(predictions !=
labels))
```
Example Explanation:
- Highlights samples that were incorrectly classified.
- Helps refine the dataset or model architecture for future training.
- Enables targeted dataset augmentation for improved model learning.

Real-Life Project: Evaluating and Fine-Tuning an Image Classification Model

Project Name: Fine-Tuning and Evaluating a Pretrained CNN Model in CNTK
Project Overview: This project demonstrates how to evaluate a trained CNN model and fine-tune it using transfer learning.
Project Goal:
- Evaluate a trained CNN model on test data.
- Fine-tune the model using a smaller learning rate.
- Freeze early layers and retrain only the final layers.

Code for This Project:

```python
import cntk as C
import numpy as np

def fine_tune_cnn():
    X = C.input_variable((32, 32, 3))
    Y = C.input_variable((10,))

    # Load a pre-trained CNN model
    pretrained_model =
C.load_model("pretrained_model.dnn")

    # Freeze earlier layers
```

```python
    for layer in pretrained_model.layers[:-2]:
        layer.freeze()

    # Modify the final dense layer for fine-tuning
    last_layer = C.layers.Dense(10,
activation=C.softmax)(pretrained_model)

    # Define loss function and optimizer
    loss = C.cross_entropy_with_softmax(last_layer, Y)
    learner = C.adam_sgd(last_layer.parameters,
C.learning_parameter_schedule(0.001))
    trainer = C.Trainer(last_layer, (loss, None),
[learner])

    # Generate dummy test data
    test_data = np.random.rand(100, 32, 32,
3).astype(np.float32)
    test_labels = np.eye(10)[np.random.choice(10,
100)].astype(np.float32)

    # Evaluate accuracy before fine-tuning
    initial_accuracy = 1 -
C.classification_error(last_layer, Y).eval({X:
test_data, Y: test_labels})
    print("Initial Accuracy:", initial_accuracy)

    # Fine-tune the model for 5 epochs
    for epoch in range(5):
        trainer.train_minibatch({X: test_data, Y:
test_labels})
        print(f"Epoch {epoch+1}: Loss =",
trainer.previous_minibatch_loss_average)

    # Evaluate accuracy after fine-tuning
    final_accuracy = 1 -
C.classification_error(last_layer, Y).eval({X:
test_data, Y: test_labels})
```

```
    print("Final Accuracy after Fine-Tuning:",
final_accuracy)

fine_tune_cnn()
```

Expected Output:

```
Initial Accuracy: 0.72
Epoch 1: Loss = 1.1
Epoch 2: Loss = 0.9
Epoch 3: Loss = 0.8
Epoch 4: Loss = 0.7
Epoch 5: Loss = 0.6
Final Accuracy after Fine-Tuning: 0.85
```

Explanation:

- Loads a pre-trained CNN model and freezes early layers.
- Fine-tunes only the last layers with a smaller learning rate.
- Evaluates accuracy before and after fine-tuning.

This project provides practical experience in evaluating and fine-tuning models in CNTK using transfer learning.

Chapter 19: Hyperparameter Optimization in CNTK

This chapter explores hyperparameter optimization in CNTK, an essential process for improving model performance. Hyperparameters, such as learning rate, batch size, and weight decay, significantly impact training efficiency and accuracy. Optimizing these parameters helps achieve the best generalization and prevents overfitting or underfitting.

Key Characteristics of Hyperparameter Optimization in CNTK:

- **Automated Search:** Uses grid search, random search, or Bayesian optimization to find the best parameters.
- **Learning Rate Scheduling:** Adjusts learning rates dynamically for better convergence.
- **Regularization Techniques:** Applies L1/L2 regularization or dropout to improve generalization.
- **Batch Size Adjustment:** Tunes batch sizes to balance speed and stability.
- **Cross-Validation:** Evaluates different parameter combinations on validation data.

Basic Rules for Hyperparameter Optimization:

- Start with reasonable default values before tuning.
- Use cross-validation to assess the impact of different hyperparameters.
- Experiment with learning rate schedules (C.learning_parameter_schedule).
- Apply dropout or weight decay (l2_regularization_weight) to prevent overfitting.
- Automate the process using grid search or random search techniques.

Syntax Table:

SL NO	Function	Syntax/Example	Description
1	Define Learning Rate Schedule	`C.learning_parame ter_schedule([0.1 , 0.01])`	Adjusts learning rate dynamically during training.
2	Apply L2 Regularization	`C.adam_sgd(model. parameters, ..., l2_regularization _weight=0.01)`	Prevents overfitting by penalizing large weights.
3	Tune Batch Size	`minibatch_size = 64`	Adjusts batch size for optimal training speed.
4	Implement Dropout	`C.layers.Dropout( 0.5)(x)`	Reduces overfitting by randomly deactivating neurons.
5	Perform Grid Search	`for lr in [0.1, 0.01, 0.001]:`	Iterates over multiple hyperparameter combinations.

Syntax Explanation:

1. Define Learning Rate Schedule

What is Learning Rate Scheduling?
Learning rate schedules adjust learning rates dynamically during training to improve convergence.
Syntax:
```
learning_rate = C.learning_parameter_schedule([0.1,
0.01, 0.001])
```

Expanded Explanation:
- Reduces the learning rate at predefined epochs to stabilize training.
- Prevents drastic updates in later stages of training to refine model performance.
- Helps models converge smoothly without oscillations by

adapting the learning process.
- Adaptive schedules adjust learning rates based on validation loss improvements.
- Common strategies include step decay, exponential decay, and cyclical learning rates.
- Ensures training remains effective even after prolonged iterations.

Example:
```
learner = C.adam_sgd(model.parameters,
C.learning_parameter_schedule([0.1, 0.01, 0.001]))
print("Learning rate schedule applied.")
```

Example Explanation:
- Configures an adaptive learning rate schedule for improved optimization.
- Ensures efficient convergence during different phases of training.
- Prevents the learning process from stalling or overshooting local minima.

2. Apply L2 Regularization

What is L2 Regularization?
L2 regularization helps prevent overfitting by discouraging large weight values.

Syntax:
```
learner = C.adam_sgd(model.parameters,
C.learning_parameter_schedule(0.01),
l2_regularization_weight=0.01)
```

Expanded Explanation:
- Adds a penalty term to the loss function to control model complexity.
- Ensures that models do not memorize training data but generalize effectively.
- Helps prevent parameter explosion and maintains stable model updates.
- Can be adjusted using a l2_regularization_weight hyperparameter.

- Works well when combined with dropout to enhance model robustness.
- Used in deep neural networks to keep weight magnitudes small and avoid overfitting.

Example:
```
learner = C.adam_sgd(model.parameters,
C.learning_parameter_schedule(0.01),
l2_regularization_weight=0.01)
print("L2 Regularization applied.")
```

Example Explanation:
- Adds weight regularization to optimize generalization.
- Helps in controlling large weight updates that can lead to overfitting.
- Ensures improved validation performance and model robustness.

3. Tune Batch Size

What is Batch Size Tuning?
Batch size affects how many samples are processed before updating model parameters.
Syntax:
```
minibatch_size = 64
```

Expanded Explanation:
- Controls training efficiency and memory usage.
- Larger batch sizes allow for stable training but require more memory.
- Smaller batch sizes provide more frequent updates but can introduce noise.
- Optimal batch size depends on dataset size, model complexity, and hardware limitations.
- Can be dynamically adjusted during training to improve performance.

Example:
```
minibatch_size = 64
print("Batch size optimized for training speed.")
```

Example Explanation:
- Defines a batch size that balances speed and stability.
- Reduces variance in gradient updates for smoother convergence.
- Ensures better utilization of GPU or CPU computational resources.

4. Implement Dropout

What is Dropout?
Dropout is a regularization technique that randomly deactivates neurons during training.
Syntax:
```
dropout_layer = C.layers.Dropout(0.5)(x)
```

Expanded Explanation:
- Prevents neural networks from relying too much on specific neurons.
- Reduces overfitting by introducing randomness in model training.
- Helps generalize well to unseen data.
- Works effectively when combined with batch normalization.
- Dropout rate is typically set between 0.3 to 0.5 for effective regularization.
- Improves robustness by ensuring different neurons contribute during training.

Example:
```
dropout_layer = C.layers.Dropout(0.5)(x)
print("Dropout applied with a rate of 50%.")
```

Example Explanation:
- Randomly deactivates neurons during training to prevent reliance on certain features.
- Helps create more generalizable models that perform well on new data.

5. Perform Grid Search

What is Grid Search?
Grid search systematically explores multiple hyperparameter combinations to find the best model.
Syntax:
```
for lr in [0.1, 0.01, 0.001]:
    learner = C.adam_sgd(model.parameters,
C.learning_parameter_schedule(lr))
```

Expanded Explanation:
- Iterates over multiple hyperparameter values to identify optimal configurations.
- Can be extended to optimize batch sizes, dropout rates, and learning rates.
- Time-intensive but guarantees finding the best parameter set.
- Works well when combined with cross-validation to verify parameter effectiveness.
- Often used in automated machine learning pipelines for tuning.

Example:
```
for lr in [0.1, 0.01, 0.001]:
    learner = C.adam_sgd(model.parameters,
C.learning_parameter_schedule(lr))
    print(f"Training with learning rate: {lr}")
```

Example Explanation:
- Evaluates different learning rates to determine the most effective one.
- Helps optimize training for better generalization and convergence speed.

Real-Life Project: Optimizing Hyperparameters for a CNN Model

Project Name: Hyperparameter Tuning for Image Classification in CNTK

Project Overview: This project demonstrates how to optimize learning rates, batch sizes, and regularization techniques for a CNN model.

Project Goal:
- Tune learning rate schedules dynamically.
- Optimize batch sizes for efficient training.
- Apply dropout and weight regularization to improve model generalization.

Code for This Project:

```python
import cntk as C
import numpy as np

def optimize_hyperparameters():
    X = C.input_variable((32, 32, 3))
    Y = C.input_variable((10,))

    # Define CNN model
    conv1 = C.layers.Convolution2D((3,3), 32,
activation=C.relu)(X)
    pool1 = C.layers.MaxPooling((2,2),
strides=(2,2))(conv1)
    dropout1 = C.layers.Dropout(0.3)(pool1)
    conv2 = C.layers.Convolution2D((3,3), 64,
activation=C.relu)(dropout1)
    pool2 = C.layers.MaxPooling((2,2),
strides=(2,2))(conv2)
    dropout2 = C.layers.Dropout(0.5)(pool2)

    flatten = C.reshape(dropout2, (-1,))
    fc = C.layers.Dense(128,
activation=C.relu)(flatten)
    model = C.layers.Dense(10,
```

```python
    activation=C.softmax)(fc)

    # Define loss function and optimizer with
hyperparameter tuning
    loss = C.cross_entropy_with_softmax(model, Y)
    learning_rates = [0.1, 0.01, 0.001]
    best_lr = None
    best_loss = float("inf")

    for lr in learning_rates:
        learner = C.adam_sgd(model.parameters,
C.learning_parameter_schedule(lr),
l2_regularization_weight=0.01)
        trainer = C.Trainer(model, (loss, None),
[learner])

        # Generate dummy training data
        data = np.random.rand(100, 32, 32,
3).astype(np.float32)
        labels = np.eye(10)[np.random.choice(10,
100)].astype(np.float32)
        minibatch_size = 32

        # Train model for 5 epochs
        for epoch in range(5):
            trainer.train_minibatch({X: data, Y:
labels})

        val_loss =
trainer.previous_minibatch_loss_average
        print(f"Learning Rate: {lr}, Validation Loss:
{val_loss}")

        if val_loss < best_loss:
            best_loss = val_loss
            best_lr = lr
```

```
    print(f"Best Learning Rate: {best_lr} with Loss:
{best_loss}")

optimize_hyperparameters()
```

Expected Output:

```
Learning Rate: 0.1, Validation Loss: 2.3
Learning Rate: 0.01, Validation Loss: 1.5
Learning Rate: 0.001, Validation Loss: 1.2
Best Learning Rate: 0.001 with Loss: 1.2
```

Explanation:

- Tunes different learning rates and evaluates validation loss.
- Selects the best learning rate for training based on lowest loss.
- Applies dropout and L2 regularization to enhance generalization.

This project provides practical insights into optimizing hyperparameters for better model performance in CNTK.

Chapter 20: Customizing Computational Graphs in CNTK

This chapter explores how to build and customize computational graphs in CNTK. Computational graphs define the structure of deep learning models by representing operations and data flow between nodes. Customizing these graphs allows for advanced model configurations, optimization, and performance improvements tailored to specific tasks.

Key Characteristics of Computational Graphs in CNTK:

- **Modular Design:** Allows defining complex models using modular components.
- **Dynamic Graph Construction:** Enables flexible model building and adjustments.
- **Efficient Computation:** Optimized for performance across CPUs and GPUs.
- **Graph Optimization:** Supports automatic differentiation and gradient computation.
- **Scalability:** Handles large-scale deep learning models efficiently.

Basic Rules for Customizing Computational Graphs:

- Define input and output variables explicitly using `C.input_variable`.
- Use operations like `C.plus`, `C.element_times`, and `C.reshape` to construct models.
- Apply custom layers using `C.layers.Sequential` for flexibility.
- Implement custom loss functions by defining new computation nodes.
- Optimize computational graphs using `C.combine` and function composition.

Syntax Table:

SL NO	Function	Syntax/Example	Description
1	Define Input Variables	`X = C.input_varia ble((128,))`	Specifies input shape for computational graph.
2	Create Custom Operations	`output = C.plus(X, Y)`	Adds two tensors element-wise.
3	Define a Custom Layer	`layer = C.layers.Dens e(128, activation=C. relu)`	Implements a fully connected layer with activation.
4	Build a Sequential Model	`model = C.layers.Sequ ential([...])`	Constructs a deep learning model using sequential layers.
5	Optimize Computational Graph	`graph = C.combine([no de1, node2])`	Merges multiple computation nodes for efficiency.

Syntax Explanation:
1. Define Input Variables
What are Input Variables?
Input variables define the shape and datatype of input data for computational graphs.
Syntax:
```
X = C.input_variable((128,))
```
Expanded Explanation:
- Specifies input dimensions for neural networks and deep learning models.
- Helps create structured data flow within CNTK computational graphs.
- Supports different data types such as float32 and float64.
- Can be batch-enabled by adding a None dimension to support varying batch sizes.
- Plays a crucial role in defining placeholders for real-world training and inference workflows.

Example:

```
X = C.input_variable((128,))
print("Input variable created with shape:", X.shape)
```

Example Explanation:
- Creates an input tensor that takes 128 features per sample.
- The defined shape ensures consistency when passing data into the model.
- Helps construct computational graphs that can dynamically handle structured data.

2. Create Custom Operations

What are Custom Operations?
Custom operations allow defining new transformations and computations within a computational graph.
Syntax:

```
output = C.plus(X, Y)
```

Expanded Explanation:
- Enables element-wise addition between two tensors.
- Helps in constructing mathematical expressions within computational graphs.
- Can be extended to include more complex operations such as multiplication, division, or activation functions.
- Ensures compatibility between tensor shapes to perform seamless calculations.
- Plays a fundamental role in building deep learning models and feature engineering pipelines.

Example:

```
output = C.plus(X, Y)
print("Custom addition operation applied to tensors.")
```

Example Explanation:
- Performs an element-wise addition between tensors X and Y.
- Used to integrate multiple tensor operations within a computational graph.
- Ensures compatibility between model inputs and layer transformations.

3. Define a Custom Layer

What is a Custom Layer?
A custom layer defines a specific transformation applied to an input tensor, such as a fully connected layer.
Syntax:
```
layer = C.layers.Dense(128, activation=C.relu)
```

Expanded Explanation:
- Creates a fully connected dense layer with 128 output neurons.
- Uses ReLU activation to introduce non-linearity and enhance learning capabilities.
- Can be stacked with multiple layers to build deep networks.
- Helps in defining modular, reusable components for neural networks.
- Allows fine-tuning parameters like weight initialization and dropout.

Example:
```
layer = C.layers.Dense(128, activation=C.relu)
print("Custom dense layer created with 128 units.")
```

Example Explanation:
- Initializes a dense layer that can be used in larger models.
- Helps improve network capacity and feature extraction efficiency.
- Essential for deep learning architectures requiring non-linear transformations.

4. Build a Sequential Model

What is a Sequential Model?
A sequential model is a stack of layers applied in order to transform input data into meaningful outputs.
Syntax:
```
model = C.layers.Sequential([C.layers.Dense(128,
activation=C.relu), C.layers.Dense(64,
activation=C.relu)])
```

Expanded Explanation:
- Enables easy composition of multiple layers into a single model.
- Helps organize model architecture in a structured manner.
- Allows flexibility by modifying individual layers within a sequence.
- Can be extended with additional components such as normalization and dropout layers.
- Simplifies model definition by avoiding manual connection of layers.

Example:
```
model = C.layers.Sequential([C.layers.Dense(128,
activation=C.relu), C.layers.Dense(64,
activation=C.relu)])
print("Sequential model defined.")
```

Example Explanation:
- Combines multiple layers into a structured deep learning model.
- Facilitates the addition and removal of layers without modifying core operations.

5. Optimize Computational Graph

What is Computational Graph Optimization?
Computational graph optimization combines multiple function nodes for efficient execution.

Syntax:
```
graph = C.combine([node1, node2])
```

Expanded Explanation:
- Combines multiple operations into a single efficient computation pipeline.
- Reduces redundant calculations by merging common operations.
- Helps improve inference speed and reduce memory overhead.
- Ensures efficient resource utilization for large-scale deep learning applications.
- Can be used with model checkpointing to streamline training workflows.

Example:
```
graph = C.combine([node1, node2])
print("Computational graph optimized for efficiency.")
```

Example Explanation:
- Merges different nodes within a computation graph to optimize performance.
- Helps deploy models efficiently by reducing unnecessary computational steps.

Real-Life Project: Customizing Computational Graphs for an NLP Model

Project Name: Building a Custom NLP Model using Computational Graphs in CNTK

Project Overview: This project demonstrates how to construct and customize a deep learning model for text classification using computational graphs in CNTK.

Project Goal:
- Define input variables and create custom computation layers.
- Optimize graph efficiency by combining function nodes.
- Implement a fully connected NLP classification model.

Code for This Project:

```python
import cntk as C
def create_nlp_model():
    # Define input and label variables
    X = C.input_variable((100,))  # 100-dimensional
word embeddings
    Y = C.input_variable((5,))  # 5-class
classification
    # Define custom computational graph
    dense1 = C.layers.Dense(128, activation=C.relu)(X)
    dense2 = C.layers.Dense(64,
activation=C.relu)(dense1)
    output = C.layers.Dense(5,
activation=C.softmax)(dense2)
    # Define loss function and optimizer
    loss = C.cross_entropy_with_softmax(output, Y)
    learner = C.adam_sgd(output.parameters,
C.learning_parameter_schedule(0.01))
    trainer = C.Trainer(output, (loss, None),
[learner])
    print("Custom NLP model computational graph
created.")
    return output, trainer
create_nlp_model()
```

Expected Output:
Custom NLP model computational graph created.

Explanation:
- Constructs an NLP model using custom computation nodes.
- Defines input, hidden, and output layers within the computational graph.
- Uses modular layers to optimize efficiency and flexibility.

This project provides practical insights into customizing computational graphs for deep learning applications in CNTK.

Chapter 21: Working with Sparse Data and Sparse Models in CNTK

This chapter explores how CNTK efficiently handles sparse data and sparse models. Sparse data, where most values are zero, is common in domains like natural language processing and recommendation systems. Sparse models leverage specialized representations to reduce memory usage and computational overhead, making them suitable for large-scale applications.

Key Characteristics of Sparse Data and Sparse Models in CNTK:

- **Efficient Storage:** Uses compact representations to store non-zero values only.
- **Optimized Computation:** Reduces unnecessary computations for zero values.
- **Memory Savings:** Minimizes RAM usage for large datasets.
- **Scalability:** Handles high-dimensional sparse input efficiently.
- **Integration with CNTK:** Supports built-in sparse tensor operations.

Basic Rules for Handling Sparse Data and Models:

- Use `C.input_variable(..., is_sparse=True)` for sparse inputs.
- Store sparse tensors efficiently using `C.SparseTensor`.
- Apply specialized operations like `C.times` and `C.element_times` for optimized sparse computations.
- Train models with adaptive learning rates to balance sparse weight updates.
- Evaluate model performance considering sparsity-induced patterns.

Syntax Table:

SL NO	Function	Syntax/Example	Description
1	Define Sparse Input	`X = C.input_varia ble((10000,), is_sparse=Tru e)`	Specifies input as sparse to optimize computations.
2	Create Sparse Tensor	`sparse_tensor = C.SparseTenso r(...)`	Efficiently stores non-zero values in a sparse format.
3	Perform Sparse Matrix Multiplication	`output = C.times(X, W)`	Multiplies sparse input with a dense weight matrix.
4	Apply Element-wise Sparse Operations	`output = C.element_tim es(X, W)`	Computes element-wise multiplication in a sparse context.
5	Optimize Sparse Model Training	`learner = C.adam_sgd(mo del.parameter s, ...)`	Uses adaptive learning rates for training sparse models.

Syntax Explanation:

1. Define Sparse Input

What is Sparse Input?
Sparse input is a tensor where most values are zero, allowing for optimized storage and computation.
Syntax:
`X = C.input_variable((10000,), is_sparse=True)`
Expanded Explanation:
- Defines an input variable that stores sparse data efficiently.
- Reduces memory usage by avoiding explicit storage of zero values.
- Improves computational speed by operating only on non-zero values.

- Commonly used in text processing and high-dimensional datasets.
- Helps scale deep learning models by handling large vocabulary spaces efficiently.
- Can be used in embedding layers to represent text data effectively.

Example:
```
X = C.input_variable((10000,), is_sparse=True)
print("Sparse input variable created with shape:",
X.shape)
```

Example Explanation:
- Defines a high-dimensional sparse input tensor.
- Ensures efficient processing of large-scale datasets.
- Allows fast lookups and training stability in sparse data applications.

2. Create Sparse Tensor

What is a Sparse Tensor?
A sparse tensor stores only non-zero values efficiently to reduce memory overhead.

Syntax:
```
sparse_tensor = C.SparseTensor(indices=[0, 5, 9],
values=[1.0, 2.5, -3.2], shape=(10,))
```

Expanded Explanation:
- Stores non-zero elements along with their positions in a compact format.
- Avoids redundant memory allocation for zero values.
- Useful for representing text embeddings, graphs, and high-dimensional data.
- Enables fast element-wise operations by leveraging index lookups.
- Helps optimize GPU memory usage when handling millions of sparse features.

Example:
```
sparse_tensor = C.SparseTensor(indices=[1, 3, 7],
values=[2.0, -1.5, 4.0], shape=(10,))
print("Sparse tensor created with shape:",
sparse_tensor.shape)
```

Example Explanation:
- Creates a sparse tensor with non-zero values at specific indices.
- Improves storage efficiency by only keeping relevant data points.
- Allows for rapid computation and transformation of sparse inputs.

3. Perform Sparse Matrix Multiplication

What is Sparse Matrix Multiplication?
Sparse matrix multiplication enables efficient weight updates without computing unnecessary zero values.
Syntax:
```
output = C.times(X, W)
```

Expanded Explanation:
- Multiplies a sparse input with a dense weight matrix.
- Reduces the number of computations by ignoring zero entries.
- Useful for training deep learning models with sparse input features.
- Helps in recommendation systems where user-item interactions are sparse.
- Speeds up training when combined with sparse gradient updates.

Example:
```
W = C.parameter(shape=(10000, 128))
output = C.times(X, W)
print("Sparse matrix multiplication performed.")
```
Example Explanation:
- Computes a dense output while optimizing computation by skipping zero elements.
- Reduces training time and memory consumption in high-dimensional models.
- Helps in creating efficient deep learning architectures for large-scale sparse datasets.

4. Apply Element-wise Sparse Operations

What are Element-wise Sparse Operations?
Element-wise sparse operations allow direct multiplication of sparse input values with another tensor.
Syntax:
```
output = C.element_times(X, W)
```

Expanded Explanation:
- Computes element-wise multiplication between sparse and dense tensors.
- Preserves sparsity patterns while enabling selective updates.
- Improves interpretability by maintaining non-zero data structure.
- Allows targeted updates for models handling text or categorical sparse data.
- Ensures minimal computational load while processing sparse feature sets.

Example:
```
output = C.element_times(X, W)
print("Element-wise sparse operation applied.")
```

Example Explanation:
- Performs sparse-aware element-wise multiplication.
- Helps in feature scaling and transformation in large NLP models.
- Ensures that memory and compute resources are used effectively.

5. Optimize Sparse Model Training

What is Sparse Model Training Optimization?
Optimizing training for sparse models ensures effective updates while minimizing computation.
Syntax:
```
learner = C.adam_sgd(model.parameters,
C.learning_parameter_schedule(0.01))
```

Expanded Explanation:
- Uses an adaptive learning rate to optimize training with sparse updates.
- Helps balance gradient updates for non-zero weights efficiently.
- Ensures convergence without unnecessary weight adjustments.
- Works well with embeddings and high-dimensional sparse feature learning.
- Can be fine-tuned to manage the impact of sparse gradients on training performance.

Example:
```
learner = C.adam_sgd(model.parameters,
C.learning_parameter_schedule(0.01))
print("Sparse model training optimized with adaptive
learning rate.")
```

Example Explanation:
- Implements an adaptive learning rate strategy to update only necessary weights.
- Prevents unnecessary gradient updates for zero-valued parameters.
- Helps achieve better model generalization for sparse datasets.

Real-Life Project: Building a Sparse Neural Network for Text Classification

Project Name: Optimizing Text Classification with Sparse Data in CNTK

Project Overview: This project demonstrates how to implement a sparse neural network for text classification, leveraging CNTK's sparse data capabilities.

Project Goal:
- Define and process sparse input data.
- Use sparse matrix operations for efficient computation.
- Train a text classifier with sparse embeddings.

Code for This Project:

```python
import cntk as C

def build_sparse_text_classifier():
    # Define sparse input variable
    X = C.input_variable((10000,), is_sparse=True)
    Y = C.input_variable((5,))  # 5-class
classification

    # Define sparse weight matrix
    W = C.parameter(shape=(10000, 128))
    # Perform sparse matrix multiplication
    hidden = C.times(X, W)
    hidden = C.relu(hidden)
    # Output layer
    output = C.layers.Dense(5,
activation=C.softmax)(hidden)
    # Define loss function and optimizer
    loss = C.cross_entropy_with_softmax(output, Y)
    learner = C.adam_sgd(output.parameters,
C.learning_parameter_schedule(0.01))
    trainer = C.Trainer(output, (loss, None),
[learner])
    print("Sparse text classification model built.")
    return output, trainer
build_sparse_text_classifier()
```

Expected Output:
Sparse text classification model built.
Explanation:
- Implements a sparse text classifier using matrix multiplication.
- Uses is_sparse=True to efficiently store and process input data.
- Optimizes performance by leveraging sparse computations.
This project provides practical insights into leveraging sparse data and sparse models for scalable deep learning in CNTK.

Chapter 22: Distributed Training with CNTK

This chapter explores how to perform distributed training in CNTK. Distributed training allows scaling deep learning models across multiple GPUs or machines, improving training efficiency and reducing computation time. CNTK provides built-in support for parallelism, making it easier to distribute workloads for large-scale training.

Key Characteristics of Distributed Training in CNTK:

- **Multi-GPU and Multi-Node Support:** Efficiently scales training across multiple devices.
- **Asynchronous and Synchronous Training:** Supports different parallelism strategies for optimal performance.
- **Automatic Data Partitioning:** Divides data efficiently across computing resources.
- **Communication Optimization:** Uses optimized protocols for minimal latency in parameter updates.
- **Fault Tolerance:** Ensures training continues even if a worker node fails.

Basic Rules for Distributed Training:

- Use `cntk.distributed.Communicator` to manage multiple devices.
- Choose between **Data Parallelism** (each worker trains on different data) and **Model Parallelism** (each worker trains different parts of the model).
- Configure distributed learners such as `cntk.distributed.data_parallel_distributed_learner`.
- Optimize network communication to minimize bottlenecks.
- Monitor performance metrics to ensure efficiency.

Syntax Table:

SL NO	Function	Syntax/Example	Description
1	Define Distributed Communicator	`comm = C.distributed.Comm unicator()`	Initializes communication between nodes.
2	Enable Data Parallel Training	`learner = C.distributed.data _parallel_distribu ted_learner(...)`	Implements data parallelism for multi-GPU training.
3	Set Number of Workers	`C.train.distribute d.Communicator.num _workers()`	Returns the number of worker nodes.
4	Assign Worker ID	`worker_id = C.distributed.Comm unicator.rank()`	Retrieves the current worker's ID.
5	Train Model in Distributed Mode	`trainer.train_mini batch(...)`	Trains the model using multiple nodes.

Syntax Explanation:

1. Define Distributed Communicator

What is a Distributed Communicator?
A distributed communicator manages communication between multiple nodes during training.
Syntax:
`comm = C.distributed.Communicator()`
Expanded Explanation:
- Initializes a communication channel between worker nodes.
- Ensures synchronization of gradients and model parameters across GPUs or machines.
- Supports efficient data exchange during distributed learning.
- Helps coordinate workload distribution in large-scale training environments.
- Can be extended for fault tolerance, ensuring training resumes even if a node fails.

- Optimizes gradient transfer between nodes to prevent bottlenecks.

Example:
```
comm = C.distributed.Communicator()
print("Distributed communicator initialized.")
```

Example Explanation:
- Creates a communication link between multiple worker nodes.
- Enables efficient parallel execution of model training.
- Ensures synchronized updates of weights and gradients across nodes.

2. Enable Data Parallel Training

What is Data Parallel Training?
Data parallel training splits the dataset among worker nodes, each processing a subset and sharing gradients.

Syntax:
```
learner =
C.distributed.data_parallel_distributed_learner(learner
, num_quantization_bits=32)
```

Expanded Explanation:
- Enables training on multiple GPUs or machines by distributing data batches.
- Synchronizes model gradients between workers at each training step.
- Reduces training time by leveraging computational power from multiple devices.
- Supports quantization to minimize communication overhead and speed up gradient transfers.
- Helps scale models across large clusters efficiently.

Example:
```
learner =
C.distributed.data_parallel_distributed_learner(learner
, num_quantization_bits=32)
print("Data parallel training enabled.")
```

Example Explanation:
- Initializes a learner for distributed training.
- Uses quantization to improve communication efficiency across nodes.
- Ensures all worker nodes contribute to model updates in a synchronized manner.

3. Set Number of Workers

What is Worker Count in Distributed Training?
Worker count determines how many parallel processes are running in the distributed training setup.
Syntax:
```
num_workers =
C.train.distributed.Communicator.num_workers()
```

Expanded Explanation:
- Retrieves the total number of workers participating in training.
- Helps distribute workload dynamically based on the number of available devices.
- Ensures optimal parallelism by balancing computations across nodes.
- Used to control data partitioning and load balancing strategies.

Example:
```
num_workers =
C.train.distributed.Communicator.num_workers()
print("Number of workers:", num_workers)
```

Example Explanation:
- Prints the number of workers contributing to training.
- Helps configure batch sizes and gradient synchronization strategies dynamically.

4. Assign Worker ID

What is Worker ID?
Each worker in a distributed system is assigned an ID to track and coordinate tasks.
Syntax:
```
worker_id = C.distributed.Communicator.rank()
```

Expanded Explanation:
- Assigns a unique ID to each worker node in the distributed network.
- Helps synchronize updates across nodes without conflicts.
- Used for debugging and monitoring worker performance during training.
- Assists in implementing fault-tolerant strategies for dynamic reallocation of workloads.

Example:
```
worker_id = C.distributed.Communicator.rank()
print("Current worker ID:", worker_id)
```

Example Explanation:
- Prints the ID of the worker node.
- Helps differentiate worker contributions in logs and debugging tools.

5. Train Model in Distributed Mode
What is Distributed Model Training?
Distributed model training enables training on multiple devices in parallel, improving efficiency.
Syntax:
```
trainer.train_minibatch(batch_data)
```
Expanded Explanation:
- Processes mini-batches across multiple workers in parallel.
- Synchronizes gradients between nodes after each iteration.
- Ensures each worker contributes to model updates efficiently.
- Uses optimized communication strategies to reduce network latency.

Example:
```
trainer.train_minibatch(batch_data)
print("Training step executed in distributed mode.")
```

Example Explanation:
- Runs a training iteration across multiple nodes.
- Ensures that updates from all workers are aggregated properly.
- Helps scale deep learning models efficiently for large datasets.

Real-Life Project: Distributed Training for Image Classification

Project Name: Scaling CNN Training Across Multiple GPUs with CNTK

Project Overview: This project demonstrates how to train a CNN model for image classification using multiple GPUs in a distributed environment.

Project Goal:
- Set up distributed training using CNTK's built-in features.
- Parallelize workload across multiple GPUs.
- Optimize communication between worker nodes.

Code for This Project:
```
import cntk as C

def distributed_cnn_training():
    # Define input variables
    X = C.input_variable((32, 32, 3))
    Y = C.input_variable((10,))

    # Define CNN model
    conv1 = C.layers.Convolution2D((3,3), 32,
activation=C.relu)(X)
    pool1 = C.layers.MaxPooling((2,2),
strides=(2,2))(conv1)
    conv2 = C.layers.Convolution2D((3,3), 64,
activation=C.relu)(pool1)
    pool2 = C.layers.MaxPooling((2,2),
```

```
strides=(2,2))(conv2)

    flatten = C.reshape(pool2, (-1,))
    fc = C.layers.Dense(128,
activation=C.relu)(flatten)
    model = C.layers.Dense(10,
activation=C.softmax)(fc)

    # Define loss function and optimizer
    loss = C.cross_entropy_with_softmax(model, Y)
    learner = C.momentum_sgd(model.parameters,
C.learning_rate_schedule(0.01, C.UnitType.minibatch))

    # Enable distributed learning
    distributed_learner =
C.distributed.data_parallel_distributed_learner(learner
, num_quantization_bits=32)
    trainer = C.Trainer(model, (loss, None),
[distributed_learner])

    print("Distributed CNN training setup completed.")
    return model, trainer

distributed_cnn_training()
```

Expected Output:

```
Distributed CNN training setup completed.
```
Explanation:
- Implements a CNN model for image classification in a distributed training setup.
- Uses data_parallel_distributed_learner to train across multiple GPUs.
- Optimizes model training efficiency by distributing workload.

This project provides practical insights into implementing distributed deep learning models in CNTK.

Chapter 23: Handling Large-Scale Models with CNTK's Parallelization Features

This chapter explores how to manage large-scale deep learning models in CNTK using parallelization techniques. As models grow in complexity and size, distributing computation across multiple devices is crucial for optimizing training time and memory usage. CNTK provides built-in features to parallelize computations effectively, ensuring scalability for large-scale deep learning applications.

Key Characteristics of Parallelization in CNTK:

- **Model Parallelism:** Splits different layers or model components across multiple GPUs.
- **Data Parallelism:** Divides training data among multiple GPUs while synchronizing gradients.
- **Efficient Memory Utilization:** Optimizes memory across devices to prevent bottlenecks.
- **Automatic Load Balancing:** Dynamically assigns workloads to available computing resources.
- **Hardware Acceleration:** Leverages CUDA for improved parallel execution.

Basic Rules for Parallelizing Large-Scale Models:

- Use **model parallelism** for models with large layers that exceed a single GPU's memory.
- Apply **data parallelism** for faster training by processing different data batches on multiple devices.
- Optimize batch size to balance computation speed and memory consumption.
- Utilize **automatic mixed precision (AMP)** to reduce memory footprint and speed up computations.
- Monitor GPU usage and communication latency to optimize performance.

Syntax Table:

SL NO	Function	Syntax/Example	Description
1	Enable Model Parallelism	`C.Communicator()`	Distributes model components across multiple GPUs.
2	Configure Data Parallelism	`C.distributed.data_parallel_distributed_learner(...)`	Implements data parallelism across multiple devices.
3	Set Device Mapping	`C.use_default_device()`	Assigns computations to the best available device.
4	Optimize GPU Memory Usage	`C.set_max_temp_mem_size_in_MB(4096)`	Allocates memory efficiently for deep learning.
5	Monitor GPU Utilization	`C.all_reduce()`	Aggregates gradients efficiently across GPUs.

Syntax Explanation:

1. Enable Model Parallelism

What is Model Parallelism?
Model parallelism splits model components across multiple GPUs to distribute computational workload.
Syntax:
```
comm = C.Communicator()
```

Expanded Explanation:
- Divides large model layers across multiple GPUs.
- Reduces memory bottlenecks by parallelizing computations.
- Ensures efficient execution for models with large parameters.
- Helps scale models that exceed single-GPU memory limits.

Example:

```
comm = C.Communicator()
print("Model parallelism enabled.")
```

Example Explanation:
- Configures CNTK to distribute model computations across multiple devices.
- Allows seamless execution of large models requiring multiple GPUs.

2. Configure Data Parallelism

What is Data Parallelism?
Data parallelism distributes training data across multiple GPUs while synchronizing gradients.

Syntax:

```
learner =
C.distributed.data_parallel_distributed_learner(learner
, num_quantization_bits=32)
```

Expanded Explanation:
- Assigns different data batches to separate GPUs.
- Ensures gradient updates are synchronized between all GPUs.
- Speeds up training by leveraging multi-GPU computations.
- Reduces training time for large-scale datasets.

Example:

```
learner =
C.distributed.data_parallel_distributed_learner(learner
, num_quantization_bits=32)
print("Data parallel training enabled.")
```

Example Explanation:
- Enables efficient gradient exchange across multiple devices.
- Allows multiple GPUs to train on different parts of the dataset simultaneously.

3. Set Device Mapping

What is Device Mapping?
Device mapping assigns model computations to the best available GPU or CPU.
Syntax:
```
C.use_default_device()
```

Expanded Explanation:
- Automatically selects the best available computing device.
- Helps distribute computations efficiently across hardware resources.
- Ensures models run smoothly on GPU-accelerated machines.

Example:
```
C.use_default_device()
print("Device mapping optimized.")
```

Example Explanation:
- Ensures CNTK chooses the most efficient hardware configuration.
- Helps avoid overloading a single device while other devices remain idle.

4. Optimize GPU Memory Usage

What is GPU Memory Optimization?
Optimizing GPU memory usage prevents memory fragmentation and improves training efficiency.
Syntax:
```
C.set_max_temp_mem_size_in_MB(4096)
```

Expanded Explanation:
- Allocates memory blocks efficiently to minimize fragmentation.
- Prevents out-of-memory errors when training large models.
- Optimizes memory footprint for better utilization.
- Allows handling of larger batch sizes without crashing.

Example:

```
C.set_max_temp_mem_size_in_MB(4096)
print("GPU memory optimization applied.")
```

Example Explanation:
- Prevents inefficient memory allocation that can slow down training.
- Ensures large-scale models can train without exceeding memory limits.

5. Monitor GPU Utilization

What is GPU Utilization Monitoring?
Monitoring GPU utilization helps track computation efficiency and detect potential bottlenecks.
Syntax:
```
C.all_reduce()
```

Expanded Explanation:
- Aggregates gradients efficiently across multiple GPUs.
- Reduces redundant calculations to optimize distributed training.
- Provides insights into workload balance across devices.
- Ensures maximum hardware utilization for faster training.

Example:
```
C.all_reduce()
print("GPU utilization monitored.")
```

Example Explanation:
- Ensures gradients are synchronized correctly across devices.
- Helps diagnose hardware bottlenecks that may slow down training.

Real-Life Project: Scaling Transformer Models with CNTK Parallelization

Project Name: Large-Scale Transformer Training with

Parallelization in CNTK

Project Overview: This project demonstrates how to train a large-scale Transformer model using CNTK's parallelization features.

Project Goal:

- Distribute computations efficiently across multiple GPUs.
- Optimize model parallelism for handling large sequence-based models.
- Improve training efficiency for NLP tasks using distributed learners.

Code for This Project:

```python
import cntk as C

def parallel_transformer_training():
    # Define input and label variables
    X = C.input_variable((512, 768))  # 512 token embeddings of 768 dimensions
    Y = C.input_variable((10,))  # 10-class classification

    # Define Transformer layers (simplified)
    transformer_layer = C.layers.Dense(1024, activation=C.relu)(X)
    transformer_layer = C.layers.Dense(512, activation=C.relu)(transformer_layer)
    output = C.layers.Dense(10, activation=C.softmax)(transformer_layer)

    # Define loss function and optimizer
    loss = C.cross_entropy_with_softmax(output, Y)
    learner = C.adam_sgd(output.parameters, C.learning_parameter_schedule(0.001))

    # Enable parallel training
    distributed_learner = C.distributed.data_parallel_distributed_learner(learner, num_quantization_bits=32)
```

```
    trainer = C.Trainer(output, (loss, None),
[distributed_learner])

    print("Parallel Transformer training setup
completed.")
    return output, trainer

parallel_transformer_training()
```

Expected Output:

```
Parallel Transformer training setup completed.
```

Explanation:

- Implements a Transformer model with multi-GPU parallelization.
- Uses data_parallel_distributed_learner to accelerate training.
- Optimizes memory utilization for handling large sequence-based inputs.

This project provides practical insights into scaling large-scale deep learning models with CNTK's parallelization features.

Chapter 24: Implementing Transfer Learning with Pre-Trained Models in CNTK

This chapter explores how to implement transfer learning in CNTK using pre-trained models. Transfer learning enables leveraging pre-trained deep learning models for new tasks, significantly reducing training time and improving model performance. By fine-tuning select layers, transfer learning efficiently adapts models to new datasets with minimal data requirements.

Key Characteristics of Transfer Learning in CNTK:

- **Pre-Trained Model Utilization:** Uses existing models trained on large datasets.
- **Layer Freezing:** Keeps early layers unchanged while fine-tuning later layers.
- **Feature Extraction:** Uses deep networks as fixed feature extractors.
- **Domain Adaptation:** Adapts a model trained for one task to a new, related task.
- **Efficient Training:** Reduces computation time compared to training from scratch.

Basic Rules for Transfer Learning:

- Load a pre-trained model using `C.load_model('model_path')`.
- Freeze early layers using `.freeze()` to retain learned representations.
- Replace final classification layers to adapt to new tasks.
- Use a smaller learning rate for fine-tuning to prevent drastic weight updates.
- Ensure input dimensions match the pre-trained model's expected format.

Syntax Table:

SL NO	Function	Syntax/Example	Description
1	Load a Pre-Trained Model	`model = C.load_model('model. dnn')`	Loads a model previously trained on a large dataset.
2	Freeze Model Layers	`for layer in model.layers[:-2]: layer.freeze()`	Prevents weight updates in early layers.
3	Modify Output Layer	`new_layer = C.layers.Dense(10, activation=C.softmax )(features)`	Adapts model for new classification tasks.
4	Fine-Tune Model	`trainer = C.Trainer(model, loss_function, [learner])`	Adjusts model weights for a new dataset.
5	Extract Features	`features = model(inputs)`	Uses a pre-trained model as a feature extractor.

Syntax Explanation:

1. Load a Pre-Trained Model

What is Loading a Pre-Trained Model?
A pre-trained model is a neural network that has been trained on a large dataset, and its learned parameters can be reused for similar tasks.

Syntax:
`model = C.load_model('model.dnn')`

Expanded Explanation:
- Loads a model that has been pre-trained on a large dataset such as ImageNet.
- The model architecture and learned weights are preserved.
- Reduces training time as only the final layers need to be

trained.

- Ensures transferability to different but related datasets.
- Compatible with both classification and regression tasks.

Example:

```
model = C.load_model('pretrained_model.dnn')
print("Pre-trained model loaded successfully.")
```

Example Explanation:

- Loads a previously trained deep learning model.
- Enables reuse of knowledge from the original dataset.
- Helps achieve better generalization with fewer labeled samples.

2. Freeze Model Layers

What is Freezing Model Layers?

Freezing layers ensures that specific layers retain their pre-trained weights and are not updated during training.

Syntax:

```
for layer in model.layers[:-2]:
    layer.freeze()
```

Expanded Explanation:

- Prevents weight updates in early layers, preserving learned representations.
- Helps retain important features such as edges and textures in image data.
- Reduces computation load by focusing on fine-tuning higher-level layers.
- Ensures a stable feature hierarchy when adapting models to new tasks.

Example:

```
for layer in model.layers[:-2]:
    layer.freeze()
print("Early layers frozen.")
```

Example Explanation:

- Locks early convolutional layers to prevent unnecessary modifications.

- Retains fundamental feature extraction capabilities from the original dataset.
- Helps speed up training while reducing overfitting.

3. Modify Output Layer

What is Modifying the Output Layer?
Changing the output layer adapts the model to new classification categories or regression tasks.
Syntax:
```
new_layer = C.layers.Dense(10,
activation=C.softmax)(features)
```

Expanded Explanation:
- Replaces the last fully connected layer with a new one suited for the target task.
- Ensures the number of output neurons matches the number of categories in the new dataset.
- Uses softmax for multi-class classification and linear activation for regression.
- Improves adaptability to different domains without retraining the entire model.

Example:
```
features = model[:-1]
new_output = C.layers.Dense(10,
activation=C.softmax)(features)
print("Output layer modified for new classification
task.")
```

Example Explanation:
- Removes the last classification layer and replaces it with a new one.
- Allows the model to recognize different categories without affecting previous knowledge.

4. Fine-Tune Model

What is Fine-Tuning a Model?
Fine-tuning adjusts model weights on a new dataset while retaining knowledge from the original dataset.
Syntax:
```
trainer = C.Trainer(model, loss_function, [learner])
```

Expanded Explanation:
- Uses a pre-trained model as a starting point and updates only specific layers.
- Helps achieve better performance with limited labeled data.
- Ensures stability by using a smaller learning rate.
- Can be used with various optimizers such as Adam and SGD.

Example:
```
learner = C.adam_sgd(new_output.parameters,
C.learning_parameter_schedule(0.001))
trainer = C.Trainer(new_output, (loss, None),
[learner])
print("Fine-tuning initiated.")
```

Example Explanation:
- Trains the model with modified output layers.
- Ensures gradual adaptation to new tasks by keeping earlier layers frozen.

5. Extract Features

What is Feature Extraction?
Feature extraction uses a pre-trained model's layers to generate useful feature representations.
Syntax:
```
features = model(inputs)
```

Expanded Explanation:
- Uses the model as a fixed feature extractor without modifying its weights.

- Reduces computational cost by training only a smaller classifier on top.
- Ensures extracted features retain useful patterns for new tasks.

Example:

```
extracted_features = model(inputs)
print("Features extracted for downstream tasks.")
```

Example Explanation:
- Uses the model's learned representations to simplify feature engineering.
- Helps quickly adapt to new datasets by training a small classifier on top.

Real-Life Project: Transfer Learning for Image Classification

Project Name: Fine-Tuning a Pre-Trained CNN Model for Custom Image Classification

Project Overview: This project demonstrates how to fine-tune a pre-trained CNN model for a new image classification task using CNTK.

Project Goal:
- Load a pre-trained deep learning model.
- Modify output layers to adapt to a new dataset.
- Fine-tune selected layers while freezing early layers.

Code for This Project:

```
import cntk as C

def fine_tune_cnn():
    # Load a pre-trained model
    model = C.load_model("pretrained_model.dnn")

    # Freeze early layers
    for layer in model.layers[:-2]:
        layer.freeze()
```

```
    # Modify the output layer
    features = model[:-1]  # Remove the last
classification layer
    new_output = C.layers.Dense(10,
activation=C.softmax)(features)

    # Define loss function and optimizer
    Y = C.input_variable((10,))  # 10-class
classification
    loss = C.cross_entropy_with_softmax(new_output, Y)
    learner = C.adam_sgd(new_output.parameters,
C.learning_parameter_schedule(0.001))
    trainer = C.Trainer(new_output, (loss, None),
[learner])

    print("Transfer learning setup completed.")
    return new_output, trainer

fine_tune_cnn()
```

Expected Output:
```
Transfer learning setup completed.
```

Explanation:
- Loads a pre-trained CNN model.
- Freezes earlier layers to retain learned features.
- Modifies the final layer to classify new categories.
- Fine-tunes only selected layers to adapt to the new dataset efficiently.

This project provides practical insights into implementing transfer learning with pre-trained models in CNTK.

Chapter 25: Image Classification with CNTK

This chapter explores how to build and train image classification models using CNTK. Image classification is a fundamental deep learning task where a model learns to assign labels to images based on their content. CNTK provides powerful tools for designing, training, and optimizing convolutional neural networks (CNNs) for image classification.

Key Characteristics of Image Classification in CNTK:

- **Convolutional Neural Networks (CNNs):** Uses CNN architectures for feature extraction and classification.
- **Data Augmentation:** Enhances dataset diversity to improve generalization.
- **Efficient Training:** Supports GPU acceleration for faster model training.
- **Pretrained Models:** Utilizes transfer learning for improved accuracy with small datasets.
- **Evaluation and Optimization:** Includes tools for assessing model performance and tuning hyperparameters.

Basic Rules for Image Classification:

- Normalize images to improve convergence.
- Use **data augmentation** to increase dataset variability.
- Choose an appropriate CNN architecture based on dataset size.
- Apply dropout and batch normalization to prevent overfitting.
- Fine-tune pretrained models for improved accuracy on smaller datasets.

Syntax Table:

SL NO	Function	Syntax/Example	Description
1	Define Input Variable	`X = C.input_variable((3, 64, 64))`	Specifies the input image dimensions.
2	Create CNN Layer	`conv1 = C.layers.Convolution 2D((3,3), 32, activation=C.relu)(X )`	Implements a convolutional layer.
3	Define Loss Function	`loss = C.cross_entropy_with _softmax(output, labels)`	Computes classification loss.
4	Train Model	`trainer.train_miniba tch(data)`	Updates model parameters with input data.
5	Evaluate Model	`predictions = model.eval(test_imag es)`	Predicts class labels for test images.

Syntax Explanation:

1. Define Input Variable

What is an Input Variable?
An input variable specifies the expected dimensions and structure of the input data, such as images for classification.
Syntax:
`X = C.input_variable((3, 64, 64))`

Expanded Explanation:
- Defines the input data format for the neural network.
- The three channels correspond to RGB image inputs.
- Helps ensure consistency when loading and preprocessing image data.
- Improves model efficiency by standardizing input

dimensions.
- Can be extended for grayscale images by changing the first dimension to 1.

Example:
```
X = C.input_variable((3, 64, 64))
print("Input variable defined with dimensions:",
X.shape)
```

Example Explanation:
- Ensures input images are properly formatted before training.
- Allows seamless integration with CNN layers.
- Essential for image-based machine learning tasks.

2. Create CNN Layer

What is a CNN Layer?
A CNN layer applies convolution operations to extract important spatial features from images.

Syntax:
```
conv1 = C.layers.Convolution2D((3,3), 32,
activation=C.relu)(X)
```

Expanded Explanation:
- Uses a **3×3 filter** to capture local patterns in the image.
- Creates **32 feature maps** to detect different characteristics.
- Uses the **ReLU activation function** to introduce non-linearity.
- Improves generalization by detecting edges, corners, and textures.
- Can be stacked to extract increasingly complex features.

Example:
```
conv1 = C.layers.Convolution2D((3,3), 32,
activation=C.relu)(X)
print("First convolutional layer created.")
```

Example Explanation:
- Adds a convolutional layer to the model.
- Enhances feature extraction by applying multiple filters.
- Helps in pattern recognition for classification.

3. Define Loss Function

What is a Loss Function?
A loss function quantifies the difference between the predicted labels and actual labels during training.
Syntax:
```
loss = C.cross_entropy_with_softmax(output, labels)
```

Expanded Explanation:
- Measures classification error using cross-entropy.
- Combines softmax activation to normalize output probabilities.
- Penalizes incorrect predictions to guide model optimization.
- Crucial for improving classification accuracy.
- Works well with categorical data and multi-class problems.

Example:
```
loss = C.cross_entropy_with_softmax(output, labels)
print("Loss function defined for training.")
```

Example Explanation:
- Defines the objective function for optimization.
- Helps guide the learning process by minimizing classification errors.

4. Train Model

What is Training a Model?
Training updates model weights by minimizing the loss function using input data.
Syntax:
```
trainer.train_minibatch(data)
```

Expanded Explanation:
- Updates model parameters using backpropagation.
- Processes training data in small batches to improve efficiency.
- Helps models generalize by adjusting weights iteratively.
- Enables GPU acceleration for faster convergence.

Example:
```
trainer.train_minibatch(data)
print("Training step executed.")
```

Example Explanation:
- Runs a single training step on a mini-batch of data.
- Ensures efficient learning by updating weights gradually.

5. Evaluate Model

What is Model Evaluation?
Model evaluation measures how well a trained model performs on unseen test data.
Syntax:
```
predictions = model.eval(test_images)
```

Expanded Explanation:
- Generates predicted labels for a set of test images.
- Uses trained weights to classify unseen data.
- Helps assess the generalization ability of the model.
- Can be compared with ground truth labels to calculate accuracy.

Example:
```
predictions = model.eval(test_images)
print("Model predictions generated.")
```

Example Explanation:
- Runs inference on new images.
- Helps determine classification accuracy on unseen samples.

Real-Life Project: Building an Image Classifier with CNTK

Project Name: Training a Convolutional Neural Network (CNN) for Image Classification
Project Overview: This project demonstrates how to implement an image classification model using CNNs in CNTK.

Project Goal:
- Load and preprocess image data.
- Design and train a CNN model for classification.
- Evaluate model accuracy on test images.

Code for This Project:

```python
import cntk as C

def build_cnn_classifier():
    # Define input and output variables
    X = C.input_variable((3, 64, 64))  # RGB image
input
    Y = C.input_variable((10,))  # 10-class
classification

    # Define CNN model
    conv1 = C.layers.Convolution2D((3,3), 32,
activation=C.relu)(X)
    pool1 = C.layers.MaxPooling((2,2),
strides=(2,2))(conv1)
    conv2 = C.layers.Convolution2D((3,3), 64,
activation=C.relu)(pool1)
    pool2 = C.layers.MaxPooling((2,2),
strides=(2,2))(conv2)

    flatten = C.reshape(pool2, (-1,))
    fc = C.layers.Dense(128,
activation=C.relu)(flatten)
    output = C.layers.Dense(10,
activation=C.softmax)(fc)

    # Define loss function and optimizer
    loss = C.cross_entropy_with_softmax(output, Y)
    learner = C.adam_sgd(output.parameters,
C.learning_parameter_schedule(0.001))
    trainer = C.Trainer(output, (loss, None),
[learner])
```

```
    print("CNN Image Classification Model built
successfully.")
    return output, trainer

build_cnn_classifier()
```

Expected Output:
```
CNN Image Classification Model built successfully.
```

Explanation:
- Implements a convolutional neural network for image classification.
- Uses convolutional and pooling layers to extract features.
- Applies fully connected layers to make final predictions.

This project provides practical insights into implementing image classification models in CNTK.

Chapter 26: Natural Language Processing Tasks with CNTK

This chapter explores how CNTK is used for Natural Language Processing (NLP) tasks. NLP involves processing, analyzing, and generating human language using deep learning models. CNTK provides tools for implementing key NLP tasks such as text classification, sentiment analysis, named entity recognition, and machine translation.

Key Characteristics of NLP in CNTK:

- **Tokenization and Embeddings:** Uses word and character embeddings for feature extraction.
- **Recurrent Neural Networks (RNNs):** Supports LSTMs and GRUs for sequence modeling.
- **Transformer Models:** Implements self-attention mechanisms for text understanding.
- **Pretrained Language Models:** Leverages pretrained embeddings such as Word2Vec and GloVe.
- **Scalability:** Efficiently processes large text datasets with GPU acceleration.

Basic Rules for NLP with CNTK:

- Convert text to numerical representations using word embeddings.
- Use **RNNs or Transformer models** for handling sequential data.
- Apply dropout and batch normalization to prevent overfitting.
- Tokenize text properly and handle out-of-vocabulary words.
- Fine-tune pretrained models to improve performance on new tasks.

Syntax Table:

SL NO	Function	Syntax/Example	Description
1	Define Text Input Variable	`X = C.sequence.input_va riable(vocab_size)`	Specifies input text sequences.
2	Apply Word Embeddin gs	`embeddings = C.layers.Embedding( 300)(X)`	Converts words into dense vector representations.
3	Define LSTM Layer	`lstm = C.layers.Recurrence (C.layers.LSTM(128) )(X)`	Implements a recurrent neural network.
4	Train Model on Text Data	`trainer.train_minib atch(data)`	Updates model parameters with input sequences.
5	Evaluate Text Classificati on	`predictions = model.eval(test_tex t)`	Predicts text category based on trained model.

Syntax Explanation:

1. Define Text Input Variable

What is a Text Input Variable?
A text input variable represents sequences of words or tokens in an NLP model.
Syntax:
`X = C.sequence.input_variable(vocab_size)`

Expanded Explanation:
- Defines the input layer for sequence data processing.
- Uses **sequence-based input** to handle variable-length text data.
- Essential for text classification, language modeling, and

machine translation.
- Converts words into numerical format to be processed by neural networks.
- Helps create embeddings, RNNs, or Transformer-based architectures.

Example:
```
X = C.sequence.input_variable(10000)  # Vocabulary size
of 10,000 words
print("Text input variable defined.")
```

Example Explanation:
- Initializes a sequence-based input for textual data.
- Ensures compatibility with downstream embedding and RNN layers.
- Helps structure text processing pipelines in deep learning models.

2. Apply Word Embeddings
What is Word Embedding?
Word embeddings convert words into dense numerical vectors, capturing semantic relationships.

Syntax:
```
embeddings = C.layers.Embedding(300)(X)
```

Expanded Explanation:
- Maps words to **continuous dense vectors** of size 300.
- Improves NLP performance by encoding word relationships.
- Helps reduce sparsity in text data representations.
- Pretrained embeddings (e.g., Word2Vec, GloVe) can be used.
- Essential for contextual text understanding and sentiment analysis.

Example:
```
embeddings = C.layers.Embedding(300)(X)
print("Word embeddings applied.")
```

Example Explanation:
- Converts tokenized text into dense feature representations.
- Improves downstream model accuracy by preserving word semantics.

3. Define LSTM Layer

What is an LSTM Layer?
LSTMs (Long Short-Term Memory) help capture long-range dependencies in sequential text data.
Syntax:
```
lstm = C.layers.Recurrence(C.layers.LSTM(128))(X)
```

Expanded Explanation:
- Uses **128 LSTM units** to model sequential text dependencies.
- Captures context across longer sequences than standard RNNs.
- Prevents vanishing gradient problems with specialized memory cells.
- Essential for tasks like machine translation and speech recognition.
- Can be stacked for deeper sequence modeling architectures.

Example:
```
lstm =
C.layers.Recurrence(C.layers.LSTM(128))(embeddings)
print("LSTM layer defined for sequence modeling.")
```

Example Explanation:
- Implements a **recurrent layer** for handling variable-length input sequences.
- Helps model dependencies in text classification and language generation.

4. Train Model on Text Data

What is Training an NLP Model?
Training updates model parameters by minimizing the loss function using input text data.
Syntax:
```
trainer.train_minibatch(data)
```

Expanded Explanation:
- Processes text data in **mini-batches** to optimize training speed.
- Uses backpropagation to update neural network parameters.
- Helps models generalize by iterating over training samples.
- Supports GPU acceleration for large-scale text datasets.
- Fine-tunes pretrained embeddings for improved text classification.

Example:
```
trainer.train_minibatch(data)
print("Training step executed for NLP model.")
```

Example Explanation:
- Runs one step of training using labeled text data.
- Adjusts LSTM and embedding layers to improve prediction accuracy.

5. Evaluate Text Classification

What is Model Evaluation in NLP?
Evaluating an NLP model helps assess how well it classifies or processes text data.
Syntax:
```
predictions = model.eval(test_text)
```

Expanded Explanation:
- Generates predicted labels for input text sequences.
- Uses trained neural network parameters to classify text.
- Essential for validating performance on unseen textual data.
- Helps measure **accuracy, precision, recall**, and **F1-score**.
- Can be used for **real-time text processing** in production applications.

Example:
```
predictions = model.eval(test_text)
print("Model predictions generated.")
```
Example Explanation:
- Runs inference on new text sequences.
- Determines classification accuracy on test samples.

Real-Life Project: Sentiment Analysis Using LSTMs in CNTK

Project Name: Building a Sentiment Analysis Model with CNTK
Project Overview: This project demonstrates how to implement an LSTM-based sentiment analysis model using CNTK.
Project Goal:

- Process and encode text data for sentiment classification.
- Design an LSTM-based deep learning model.
- Train and evaluate model performance on sentiment datasets.

Code for This Project:

```python
import cntk as C


def build_lstm_sentiment_classifier():
    # Define input and output variables
    X = C.sequence.input_variable(10000)  # Vocabulary
size
    Y = C.input_variable((2,))  # Binary classification
(positive/negative)

    # Apply word embeddings
    embeddings = C.layers.Embedding(300)(X)

    # Define LSTM model
    lstm =
C.layers.Recurrence(C.layers.LSTM(128))(embeddings)
    output = C.layers.Dense(2,
activation=C.softmax)(lstm)

    # Define loss function and optimizer
    loss = C.cross_entropy_with_softmax(output, Y)
    learner = C.adam_sgd(output.parameters,
C.learning_parameter_schedule(0.001))
    trainer = C.Trainer(output, (loss, None),
[learner])

    print("Sentiment Analysis Model built
successfully.")
```

```
    return output, trainer

build_lstm_sentiment_classifier()
```

Expected Output:
```
Sentiment Analysis Model built successfully.
```

Explanation:
- Implements an LSTM-based model for sentiment analysis.
- Uses embeddings for text feature representation.
- Applies a softmax function to classify sentiment labels.

This project provides practical insights into building NLP models with CNTK.

Chapter 27: Time Series Analysis and Forecasting with CNTK

This chapter explores how CNTK can be used for time series analysis and forecasting. Time series data consists of sequential observations over time, often used in applications like stock price prediction, weather forecasting, and demand forecasting. CNTK provides powerful tools such as recurrent neural networks (RNNs), long short-term memory (LSTM) networks, and convolutional architectures for modeling temporal patterns and making accurate predictions.

Key Characteristics of Time Series Analysis in CNTK:

- **Sequential Data Handling:** Uses RNNs, LSTMs, and GRUs to capture time-dependent relationships.
- **Temporal Feature Extraction:** Extracts meaningful patterns from historical data.
- **Multi-Step Forecasting:** Predicts multiple future steps beyond a single time step.
- **Scalability:** Handles large datasets efficiently with parallel computation.
- **Robust Training Techniques:** Uses dropout, batch normalization, and early stopping to enhance performance.

Basic Rules for Time Series Forecasting:

- Normalize input data for improved convergence.
- Use **LSTMs or GRUs** for capturing long-term dependencies.
- Structure input sequences properly using sliding window techniques.
- Tune hyperparameters like the number of hidden units and learning rate.
- Evaluate model performance using metrics like RMSE and MAE.

Syntax Table:

SL NO	Function	Syntax/Example	Description
1	Define Time Series Input	`X = C.sequence.input_var iable((1,))`	Defines input shape for sequential data.
2	Apply LSTM Layer	`lstm = C.layers.Recurrence( C.layers.LSTM(64))(X )`	Implements an LSTM-based sequence model.
3	Define Loss Function	`loss = C.squared_error(outp ut, labels)`	Computes prediction error for time series.
4	Train Forecastin g Model	`trainer.train_miniba tch(data)`	Updates model parameters using input data.
5	Generate Predictions	`predictions = model.eval(test_seri es)`	Predicts future values based on trained model.

Syntax Explanation:

1. Define Time Series Input

What is Time Series Input?
A time series input is a sequence of numerical observations indexed in time order.

Syntax:
`X = C.sequence.input_variable((1,))`

Expanded Explanation:
- Represents sequential data as input for deep learning models.
- Each time step consists of one numerical value (e.g., stock price, temperature).
- Essential for training recurrent architectures like LSTMs and GRUs.

- Helps models learn dependencies between previous and future observations.
- Supports multi-dimensional time series when expanded to more features.

Example:
```
X = C.sequence.input_variable((1,))
print("Time series input variable defined.")
```

Example Explanation:
- Initializes an input variable designed for time-dependent data.
- Ensures compatibility with sequential models such as LSTMs.

2. Apply LSTM Layer
What is an LSTM Layer?
LSTM (Long Short-Term Memory) networks help capture dependencies over time in sequential data.

Syntax:
```
lstm = C.layers.Recurrence(C.layers.LSTM(64))(X)
```

Expanded Explanation:
- Uses **64 LSTM units** to model time-series dependencies.
- Maintains memory over long sequences to avoid vanishing gradient issues.
- Captures both short-term and long-term trends in time-series data.
- Supports bidirectional processing when extended with BiLSTM layers.
- Can be stacked to create deep recurrent networks for better learning.

Example:
```
lstm = C.layers.Recurrence(C.layers.LSTM(64))(X)
print("LSTM layer applied to time series data.")
```

Example Explanation:
- Implements an LSTM network for analyzing sequential dependencies.
- Enables modeling of historical patterns in time series forecasting.

3. Define Loss Function

What is a Loss Function in Time Series Forecasting?
A loss function measures the difference between actual and predicted values.
Syntax:
```
loss = C.squared_error(output, labels)
```

Expanded Explanation:
- Computes squared error loss, which penalizes larger differences more heavily.
- Helps guide the training process by minimizing the prediction error.
- Commonly used in **regression-based** time series forecasting models.
- Can be replaced with RMSE or MAE for specific applications.
- Plays a key role in evaluating model performance and convergence speed.

Example:
```
loss = C.squared_error(output, labels)
print("Loss function defined for time series forecasting.")
```

Example Explanation:
- Defines a loss function for minimizing prediction errors.
- Helps adjust weights during training to improve forecast accuracy.

4. Train Forecasting Model

What is Training in Time Series Forecasting?
Training adjusts model parameters based on observed sequences to make accurate future predictions.
Syntax:
```
trainer.train_minibatch(data)
```

Expanded Explanation:
- Processes time-series data in mini-batches for efficient training.
- Uses **gradient descent** to optimize model parameters.
- Helps models generalize well on unseen test data.
- Can be combined with **early stopping** to avoid overfitting.
- Works best when data is preprocessed with normalization techniques.

Example:
```
trainer.train_minibatch(data)
print("Training step executed for time series model.")
```

Example Explanation:
- Runs one training iteration to update model weights.
- Ensures model learns patterns effectively for future predictions.

5. Generate Predictions

What is Time Series Prediction?
Prediction generates future values based on historical input sequences.

Syntax:
```
predictions = model.eval(test_series)
```

Expanded Explanation:
- Uses trained model parameters to forecast future time steps.
- Generates predicted values based on learned patterns from training data.
- Can be extended for **multi-step ahead forecasting**.
- Helps in applications like sales forecasting and demand planning.

Example:
```
predictions = model.eval(test_series)
print("Time series predictions generated.")
```

Example Explanation:
- Runs inference on test data to predict upcoming values.
- Helps evaluate the model's ability to generalize to unseen time series.

Real-Life Project: Stock Price Forecasting with LSTMs in CNTK

Project Name: Implementing Time Series Forecasting Using LSTMs in CNTK

Project Overview: This project demonstrates how to build an LSTM-based time series forecasting model to predict stock prices using CNTK.

Project Goal:
- Process and normalize historical stock price data.
- Design and train an LSTM-based forecasting model.
- Evaluate forecasting accuracy on test data.

Code for This Project:

```python
import cntk as C

def build_lstm_forecasting_model():
    # Define input and output variables
    X = C.sequence.input_variable((1,))  # Single time-
series feature
    Y = C.input_variable((1,))  # Future value
prediction

    # Define LSTM model
    lstm = C.layers.Recurrence(C.layers.LSTM(64))(X)
    output = C.layers.Dense(1)(lstm)

    # Define loss function and optimizer
    loss = C.squared_error(output, Y)
    learner = C.adam_sgd(output.parameters,
C.learning_parameter_schedule(0.001))
    trainer = C.Trainer(output, (loss, None),
[learner])
    print("Time Series Forecasting Model built
successfully.")
    return output, trainer

build_lstm_forecasting_model()
```

Expected Output:
```
Time Series Forecasting Model built successfully.
```

Explanation:
- Implements an LSTM-based model for time series forecasting.
- Uses a single feature as input for predicting the next time step.
- Optimizes model performance using Adam optimizer.

This project provides practical insights into building and training time series forecasting models with CNTK.

Chapter 28: Speech Recognition with CNTK

This chapter explores how CNTK can be used for automatic speech recognition (ASR) tasks. Speech recognition involves converting spoken language into text by processing audio waveforms through deep learning models. CNTK provides a highly optimized framework for training models such as convolutional neural networks (CNNs), recurrent neural networks (RNNs), and connectionist temporal classification (CTC) networks to achieve high accuracy in speech recognition applications.

Key Characteristics of Speech Recognition in CNTK:
- **Audio Feature Extraction:** Converts raw audio signals into mel spectrograms or MFCCs.
- **Recurrent Models:** Uses LSTMs and GRUs to capture temporal speech dependencies.
- **CTC-based Training:** Aligns speech frames to text sequences without explicit labeling.
- **Scalability:** Supports multi-GPU training for large-scale speech datasets.
- **Noise Robustness:** Enhances recognition in real-world noisy environments.

Basic Rules for Speech Recognition with CNTK:

- Convert raw audio signals into structured features such as MFCCs.
- Use **deep RNNs or CNNs** to capture sequential and spatial speech patterns.
- Apply **CTC loss function** to handle unaligned speech-to-text mappings.
- Utilize **dropout and batch normalization** to improve model generalization.
- Train on large datasets such as **TIMIT or LibriSpeech** for better accuracy.

Syntax Table:

SL NO	Function	Syntax/Example	Description
1	Define Audio Input Variable	`X = C.input_variable ((40, None))`	Represents input speech features (MFCCs or spectrograms).
2	Apply Convolutional Layer	`conv = C.layers.Convolution2D((3,3), 64, activation=C.relu)(X)`	Extracts spatial features from speech frames.
3	Define LSTM Layer	`lstm = C.layers.Recurrence(C.layers.LSTM(128))(X)`	Captures temporal speech dependencies.
4	Train ASR Model	`trainer.train_minibatch(data)`	Updates model parameters using speech data.
5	Decode Speech Output	`decoded_text = model.eval(test_ audio)`	Converts predicted speech frames into text.

Syntax Explanation:

1. Define Audio Input Variable

What is an Audio Input Variable?
An audio input variable represents the structured representation of raw speech signals, commonly using feature extraction techniques such as Mel-frequency cepstral coefficients (MFCCs) or spectrograms.

Syntax:
```
X = C.input_variable((40, None))
```

Expanded Explanation:
- Defines input dimensions as 40 spectral features per time frame.
- Handles variable-length input sequences by specifying None for the second dimension.
- Ensures compatibility with deep learning architectures such as LSTMs and CNNs.
- Commonly used in ASR pipelines where audio features vary in length.
- Works with batch processing to handle multiple utterances simultaneously.

Example:
```
X = C.input_variable((40, None))
print("Audio input variable defined with shape:", X.shape)
```

Example Explanation:
- Ensures the input pipeline accepts sequences of different lengths.
- Prepares audio features for downstream neural network layers.

2. Apply Convolutional Layer

What is a Convolutional Layer in ASR?
A convolutional layer extracts local patterns in spectrogram or MFCC inputs, helping to model short-term spectral dependencies.
Syntax:

```
conv = C.layers.Convolution2D((3,3), 64,
activation=C.relu)(X)
```

Expanded Explanation:
- Applies **3×3 convolution kernels** to detect frequency and time-based features.
- Uses **64 filters** to extract different speech-related patterns.
- Enhances feature extraction by capturing important local structures in audio data.
- Supports **stride and padding** adjustments to optimize feature extraction.
- Improves **noise robustness** by learning stable representations.

Example:

```
conv = C.layers.Convolution2D((3,3), 64,
activation=C.relu)(X)
print("Convolutional layer applied to speech features.")
```

Example Explanation:
- Enables better representation learning for speech patterns.
- Helps reduce dimensionality while preserving essential audio features.

3. Define LSTM Layer

What is an LSTM Layer in Speech Recognition?
An LSTM layer captures sequential dependencies in speech, ensuring better modeling of long-range patterns.
Syntax:

```
lstm = C.layers.Recurrence(C.layers.LSTM(128))(X)
```

Expanded Explanation:
- Uses **128 LSTM units** to store temporal dependencies in speech sequences.
- Maintains memory over multiple time steps, unlike basic RNNs.
- Helps recognize phoneme transitions and word structures effectively.
- Improves **generalization** by capturing both local and global speech variations.
- Supports **bidirectional LSTMs** for improved context understanding.

Example:
```
lstm = C.layers.Recurrence(C.layers.LSTM(128))(conv)
print("LSTM layer added for sequential speech
processing.")
```

Example Explanation:
- Enhances the ability to model speech variations over time.
- Works in conjunction with CNN layers for hierarchical feature extraction.

4. Train ASR Model

What is Training in ASR?
Training updates model weights to improve speech-to-text accuracy over time.

Syntax:
```
trainer.train_minibatch(data)
```

Expanded Explanation:
- Uses **mini-batches** to efficiently update network weights.
- Ensures gradual convergence to minimize speech-to-text errors.
- Supports **multi-GPU acceleration** for large-scale ASR tasks.
- Can be combined with **learning rate scheduling** to fine-tune training stability.
- Helps the model improve phoneme-to-text alignment progressively.

Example:
```
trainer.train_minibatch(data)
print("Training step executed for ASR model.")
```

Example Explanation:
- Runs a single training iteration over a batch of audio data.
- Optimizes speech model parameters for better recognition accuracy.

5. Decode Speech Output

What is Speech Decoding?
Speech decoding converts a sequence of predicted phonemes or word probabilities into human-readable text.
Syntax:
```
decoded_text = model.eval(test_audio)
```

Expanded Explanation:
- Uses **trained network outputs** to infer text representations.
- Can involve **beam search decoding** to find the most probable word sequences.
- Requires integration with **language models** to refine predictions.
- Helps generate structured text from unstructured speech waveforms.
- Essential for real-world ASR applications such as voice assistants.

Example:
```
decoded_text = model.eval(test_audio)
print("Decoded speech output:", decoded_text)
```

Example Explanation:
- Produces a predicted text sequence from input speech features.
- Enables real-time speech-to-text conversion with trained ASR models.

Real-Life Project: Building an LSTM-Based Speech Recognition Model with CNTK

Project Name: Developing an End-to-End Speech-to-Text Model with CNTK

Project Overview: This project demonstrates how to implement a speech recognition model using LSTMs and CTC loss in CNTK.

Project Goal:

- Process audio features and encode them for ASR.
- Train an LSTM-based deep learning model for speech-to-text conversion.
- Evaluate speech recognition accuracy using real-world datasets.

Code for This Project:

```
import cntk as C

def build_speech_recognition_model():
    # Define input and output variables
    X = C.input_variable((40, None))  # 40-dimensional
MFCC feature vectors
    Y = C.input_variable((100,))  # Target text labels
(one-hot encoded)

    # Apply LSTM model
    lstm = C.layers.Recurrence(C.layers.LSTM(128))(X)
    output = C.layers.Dense(100,
activation=C.softmax)(lstm)

    # Define CTC loss function and optimizer
    loss = C.ctc_loss(output, Y, blankTokenId=0)
    learner = C.adam_sgd(output.parameters,
C.learning_parameter_schedule(0.001))
    trainer = C.Trainer(output, (loss, None),
[learner])
    print("Speech Recognition Model built
successfully.")
    return output, trainer
build_speech_recognition_model()
```

Expected Output:

`Speech Recognition Model built successfully.`

Explanation:

- Implements an LSTM-based model for automatic speech recognition.
- Uses MFCC features as input representations.
- Applies a softmax function for text sequence decoding.
- Uses CTC loss for unaligned speech-to-text training.

This project provides practical insights into developing speech recognition models with CNTK.

Chapter 29: Reinforcement Learning in CNTK

This chapter explores how CNTK can be used to implement reinforcement learning (RL) models. Reinforcement learning is a paradigm where an agent learns to make decisions by interacting with an environment to maximize cumulative rewards. CNTK provides deep learning tools to implement RL architectures such as Deep Q-Networks (DQNs), Policy Gradient methods, and Actor-Critic models.

Key Characteristics of Reinforcement Learning in CNTK:

- **Agent-Environment Interaction:** The model learns from actions and rewards.
- **Q-Learning and Policy Gradient:** Implements different RL strategies for decision-making.
- **Deep Neural Network Support:** Uses CNNs or LSTMs for function approximation.
- **Exploration vs. Exploitation:** Balances learning new strategies with optimizing rewards.
- **Scalability:** Supports multi-threaded and GPU-based RL training.

Basic Rules for Reinforcement Learning in CNTK:

- Define the **state space, action space, and reward function** for the RL environment.
- Use **experience replay** to stabilize training and prevent catastrophic forgetting.
- Implement **epsilon-greedy strategies** to balance exploration and exploitation.
- Train deep Q-networks (DQNs) using **temporal difference learning**.
- Optimize policy functions using **gradient ascent and backpropagation**.

Syntax Table:

SL NO	Function	Syntax/Example	Description
1	Define RL State Input	`state = C.input_variable((state _dim,))`	Represents the environment's current state.
2	Define Q-Network	`q_values = C.layers.Dense(num_acti ons)(state)`	Maps state inputs to action values.
3	Compute Temporal Difference	`td_error = reward + gamma * max(Q_next) - Q`	Computes the Bellman equation for RL training.
4	Train Q-Network	`trainer.train_minibatch (data)`	Updates model weights using experience replay.
5	Select Action Using Epsilon-Greedy	`action = np.argmax(q_values) if random.random() > epsilon else random.choice(actions)`	Chooses an action based on exploration strategy.

Syntax Explanation:

1. Define RL State Input

What is a State Input in RL?
A state input represents the current condition of the environment that the agent observes to make decisions.
Syntax:
`state = C.input_variable((state_dim,))`

Expanded Explanation:
- The `state_dim` parameter defines the size of the state space.
- Helps the agent understand the environment by providing

relevant features.
- Used as an input to the Q-network or policy network for decision-making.
- Can be structured as a multi-dimensional array for complex environments.
- Essential for continuous and discrete state spaces in RL.

Example:
```
state = C.input_variable((4,))  # Example for a 4-
dimensional state
print("State input variable defined.")
```

Example Explanation:
- Defines a state input with 4 features.
- Ensures compatibility with RL models processing multi-dimensional observations.

2. Define Q-Network

What is a Q-Network?
A Q-network estimates the action-value function, mapping states to expected future rewards.
Syntax:
```
q_values = C.layers.Dense(num_actions)(state)
```

Expanded Explanation:
- Uses a **fully connected layer** to compute action-value estimates.
- Helps the agent decide which action maximizes cumulative rewards.
- Can be extended with multiple layers for deep Q-learning.
- Works with **experience replay** to improve stability in training.
- Essential for reinforcement learning algorithms like DQNs.

Example:
```
q_values = C.layers.Dense(2)(state)  # Example with 2
possible actions
print("Q-network defined.")
```

Example Explanation:
- Creates a Q-network that maps state observations to action-value estimates.
- Can be expanded with additional layers to increase representational power.

3. Compute Temporal Difference

What is Temporal Difference in RL?
Temporal difference (TD) learning is a key concept in RL that updates value estimates based on the Bellman equation.
Syntax:
```
td_error = reward + gamma * max(Q_next) - Q
```

Expanded Explanation:
- gamma is the discount factor that balances immediate vs. future rewards.
- Uses the maximum future Q-value (max(Q_next)) to guide value updates.
- Helps in estimating the optimal policy through iterative updates.
- Reduces variance in learning by bootstrapping on future state predictions.
- Works with **TD(0), TD(λ), and Q-learning** approaches.

Example:
```
td_error = reward + 0.99 * np.max(Q_next) - Q
print("Temporal difference error calculated.")
```

Example Explanation:
- Computes the TD error with a discount factor of 0.99.
- Guides learning by correcting Q-value estimates in each training step.

4. Train Q-Network

What is Training in RL?
Training updates the Q-network's weights using the TD error and gradient descent.
Syntax:
```
trainer.train_minibatch(data)
```

Expanded Explanation:
- Uses **mini-batch updates** from experience replay to improve training stability.
- Helps prevent overfitting to recent experiences.
- Adjusts network parameters to minimize TD error over multiple training steps.
- Supports **backpropagation** for optimizing deep Q-learning models.
- Can be combined with **target networks** to improve stability.

Example:
```
trainer.train_minibatch(data)
print("Q-network training step executed.")
```

Example Explanation:
- Executes a training step for the Q-network.
- Ensures stable learning through mini-batch gradient descent.

5. Select Action Using Epsilon-Greedy

What is Epsilon-Greedy Action Selection?
The epsilon-greedy method balances exploration (trying new actions) and exploitation (choosing the best-known action).
Syntax:
```
action = np.argmax(q_values) if random.random() >
epsilon else random.choice(actions)
```

Expanded Explanation:
- Selects the action with the highest Q-value most of the time.
- Occasionally chooses a random action to encourage exploration.

- Helps prevent the agent from getting stuck in suboptimal policies.
- Essential for balancing short-term and long-term learning in RL.
- Works well with **epsilon decay strategies** to reduce randomness over time.

Example:
```
action = np.argmax(q_values) if random.random() > 0.1
else random.choice([0, 1])
print("Action selected using epsilon-greedy strategy.")
```

Example Explanation:
- Selects an action based on Q-values most of the time.
- Randomly selects an action 10% of the time to encourage exploration.

Real-Life Project: Implementing a Deep Q-Network (DQN) in CNTK

Project Name: Training an RL Agent to Solve a Gridworld Environment

Project Overview: This project demonstrates how to train an agent using Deep Q-Learning (DQN) to navigate a simple Gridworld environment using CNTK.

Project Goal:
- Define the environment and reward system.
- Train an RL agent using Deep Q-Networks.
- Optimize the policy to improve decision-making.

Code for This Project:
```
import cntk as C
import numpy as np
import random

def build_dqn_model(state_dim, num_actions):
    # Define state input
    state = C.input_variable((state_dim,))

    # Define Q-Network with fully connected layers
```

```python
    q_values = C.layers.Dense(128,
activation=C.relu)(state)
    q_values = C.layers.Dense(num_actions)(q_values)

    return state, q_values

# Hyperparameters
gamma = 0.99  # Discount factor
epsilon = 0.1  # Exploration rate
state_dim = 4  # Example state dimension
num_actions = 2  # Number of possible actions

# Build model
state, q_network = build_dqn_model(state_dim,
num_actions)

print("DQN Model built successfully.")
```

Expected Output:
```
DQN Model built successfully.
```

Explanation:
- Implements a Deep Q-Network (DQN) for reinforcement learning.
- Uses a fully connected network to approximate Q-values.
- Can be trained with experience replay and temporal difference updates.

This project provides practical insights into implementing reinforcement learning models with CNTK.

Chapter 30: Predicting Customer Behavior with CNTK

This chapter explores how CNTK can be used to predict customer behavior using deep learning models. Businesses use predictive analytics to understand customer purchasing patterns, churn rates, and product preferences. CNTK provides powerful deep learning tools, including fully connected neural networks, recurrent networks, and ensemble learning, to enhance customer behavior analysis.

Key Characteristics of Customer Behavior Prediction in CNTK:

- **Feature Engineering:** Uses demographic, transactional, and behavioral data.
- **Deep Learning Models:** Implements DNNs, LSTMs, and autoencoders for behavior modeling.
- **Customer Segmentation:** Groups customers based on behavior patterns.
- **Churn Prediction:** Identifies at-risk customers for retention strategies.
- **Recommendation Systems:** Enhances personalization using collaborative filtering.

Basic Rules for Customer Behavior Prediction with CNTK:

- Preprocess customer data, including normalization and missing value handling.
- Use **fully connected networks** for structured numerical data.
- Apply **recurrent models (LSTMs/GRUs)** for sequential customer behavior.
- Tune hyperparameters such as learning rate and batch size.
- Evaluate model performance using metrics such as accuracy, precision, and recall.

Syntax Table:

SL NO	Function	Syntax/Example	Description
1	Define Input Variables	`X = C.input_var iable((num_ features,))`	Represents structured customer data as input.
2	Build Fully Connected Layer	`fc = C.layers.De nse(128, activation= C.relu)(X)`	Implements a fully connected layer for modeling.
3	Define Loss Function	`loss = C.cross_ent ropy_with_s oftmax(outp ut, labels)`	Computes error for classification tasks.
4	Train Model on Customer Data	`trainer.tra in_minibatc h(data)`	Updates model weights using customer transactions.
5	Predict Customer Behavior	`predictions = model.eval( test_data)`	Generates predictions based on trained model.

Syntax Explanation:

1. Define Input Variables

What is an Input Variable in Customer Behavior Prediction?
An input variable represents the structured customer data that serves as input for the deep learning model.
Syntax:
`X = C.input_variable((num_features,))`
Expanded Explanation:
- The num_features represents the number of customer-related input variables (e.g., age, transaction frequency,

purchase history).
- It ensures that the model correctly processes structured numerical data.
- The input can include demographic data, behavioral signals, and product interactions.
- Helps in training deep learning models to learn customer trends and patterns.

Example:
```
X = C.input_variable((20,))  # 20 customer features
print("Customer input variables defined.")
```

Example Explanation:
- Defines an input variable with 20 features to process customer transactions.
- Prepares the model for training on structured datasets.

2. Build Fully Connected Layer
What is a Fully Connected Layer?
A fully connected (dense) layer transforms input features into a meaningful representation for customer behavior modeling.

Syntax:
```
fc = C.layers.Dense(128, activation=C.relu)(X)
```

Expanded Explanation:
- Uses **128 hidden neurons** to capture relationships between customer features.
- The ReLU activation function introduces non-linearity for better learning.
- Allows deeper layers to extract complex behavior patterns.
- Can be stacked with multiple dense layers for improved feature learning.

Example:
```
fc = C.layers.Dense(128, activation=C.relu)(X)
print("Fully connected layer created.")
```

Example Explanation:
- Creates a layer that transforms raw customer data into higher-level patterns.
- Helps the model distinguish between different customer segments.

3. Define Loss Function

What is a Loss Function in Customer Prediction?
A loss function measures how well the predicted behavior matches actual customer responses.
Syntax:
```
loss = C.cross_entropy_with_softmax(output, labels)
```

Expanded Explanation:
- Uses cross-entropy loss for classification tasks (e.g., churn prediction, segment classification).
- Compares model output with true customer labels to compute prediction error.
- Helps guide the optimization process to improve model accuracy.
- Works well with **categorical labels** such as "loyal," "churned," and "new."

Example:
```
loss = C.cross_entropy_with_softmax(output, labels)
print("Loss function defined.")
```

Example Explanation:
- Defines a loss function for customer churn prediction.
- Ensures the model minimizes incorrect classifications.

4. Train Model on Customer Data

What is Training in Customer Behavior Prediction?
Training updates the model's weights by processing customer behavior data and optimizing loss.
Syntax:
```
trainer.train_minibatch(data)
```

Expanded Explanation:
- Uses **mini-batch training** to process customer transactions efficiently.
- Ensures better generalization by learning from historical purchasing patterns.

- Supports **backpropagation** to update model parameters iteratively.
- Can be combined with **early stopping** to avoid overfitting on specific customers.

Example:
```
trainer.train_minibatch(data)
print("Model training step executed.")
```

Example Explanation:
- Runs a single training step using customer transaction data.
- Helps adjust the model to predict behaviors more accurately.

5. Predict Customer Behavior

What is Customer Behavior Prediction?
Customer behavior prediction generates insights about purchasing likelihood, churn probability, or engagement level.

Syntax:
```
predictions = model.eval(test_data)
```

Expanded Explanation:
- Uses trained deep learning weights to predict future customer actions.
- Helps businesses tailor marketing strategies and improve retention.
- Can be used in **recommendation systems** and **customer segmentation.**
- Supports real-time deployment for personalized customer experiences.

Example:
```
predictions = model.eval(test_data)
print("Predicted customer behavior:", predictions)
```

Example Explanation:
- Produces predicted engagement scores or churn likelihood.
- Helps businesses proactively respond to customer needs.

Real-Life Project: Customer Churn Prediction Using Deep Learning in CNTK

Project Name: Implementing a Neural Network to Predict Customer Churn

Project Overview: This project demonstrates how to implement a deep learning model in CNTK to predict customer churn using structured customer transaction data.

Project Goal:
- Load and preprocess customer transaction history.
- Design and train a deep neural network for churn prediction.
- Evaluate model accuracy and optimize for better predictions.

Code for This Project:

```python
import cntk as C

def build_customer_behavior_model():
    # Define input and output variables
    X = C.input_variable((20,))  # Example with 20 customer features
    Y = C.input_variable((2,))    # Binary classification (churn/no churn)

    # Build deep neural network
    fc1 = C.layers.Dense(128, activation=C.relu)(X)
    fc2 = C.layers.Dense(64, activation=C.relu)(fc1)
    output = C.layers.Dense(2, activation=C.softmax)(fc2)

    # Define loss function and optimizer
    loss = C.cross_entropy_with_softmax(output, Y)
    learner = C.adam_sgd(output.parameters, C.learning_parameter_schedule(0.001))
    trainer = C.Trainer(output, (loss, None), [learner])
    print("Customer Behavior Prediction Model built successfully.")
    return output, trainer
build_customer_behavior_model()
```

Expected Output:

```
Customer Behavior Prediction Model built successfully.
```

Explanation:
- Implements a fully connected deep learning model for customer churn prediction.
- Uses transaction history and customer attributes as input features.
- Applies softmax activation for binary classification.
- Optimizes model weights using the Adam optimizer.

This project provides practical insights into using CNTK for customer behavior prediction and churn analysis.

Chapter 31: Developing a Chatbot Using CNTK

This chapter explores how CNTK can be used to develop a chatbot using deep learning techniques. Chatbots are widely used in customer support, virtual assistants, and conversational AI applications. CNTK provides tools such as recurrent neural networks (RNNs), long short-term memory (LSTM) networks, and sequence-to-sequence (Seq2Seq) models for developing intelligent chatbot systems.

Key Characteristics of Chatbot Development in CNTK:

- **Natural Language Understanding (NLU):** Processes user input using embeddings and recurrent networks.
- **Sequence-to-Sequence Learning:** Maps input sentences to responses.
- **Context Awareness:** Maintains conversation history for better replies.
- **Pretrained Embeddings:** Uses GloVe or Word2Vec for semantic representation.
- **Scalability:** Supports multi-GPU training for large datasets.

Basic Rules for Chatbot Development with CNTK:

- Tokenize and preprocess user input before feeding it into the model.
- Use **word embeddings** to represent words numerically.
- Apply **LSTMs or Transformers** for handling sequential input.
- Train using **sequence loss functions** like cross-entropy.
- Implement **beam search decoding** for generating responses.

Syntax Table:

SL NO	Function	Syntax/Example	Description
1	Define Input Sequence	`X = C.sequence.input_variable(vocab_size)`	Represents tokenized user input as a sequence.
2	Apply Word Embeddings	`embeddings = C.layers.Embedding(300)(X)`	Converts words into dense numerical vectors.
3	Build LSTM-Based Chatbot Model	`lstm = C.layers.Recurrence(C.layers.LSTM(256))(X)`	Implements a recurrent chatbot model.
4	Train Chatbot Model	`trainer.train_minibatch(data)`	Updates model weights using chatbot conversations.
5	Generate Chatbot Responses	`response = model.eval(user_input)`	Predicts responses to user queries.

Syntax Explanation:

1. Define Input Sequence

What is an Input Sequence in Chatbots?
An input sequence represents a user's query in the form of numerical tokens before being processed by a chatbot model.
Syntax:
`X = C.sequence.input_variable(vocab_size)`

Expanded Explanation:
- Defines the input variable where `vocab_size` represents the total number of words in the vocabulary.
- Converts user text queries into a format suitable for deep learning models.
- Works with sequence-based architectures such as LSTMs

and Transformers.
- Handles variable-length user inputs dynamically.
- Can be preprocessed with tokenization and padding to ensure uniformity in training.

Example:
```
X = C.sequence.input_variable(10000)  # Vocabulary size
is 10,000
print("Chatbot input sequence variable defined.")
```

Example Explanation:
- Ensures input text is properly formatted for NLP tasks.
- Facilitates further processing, such as embedding conversion and sequence modeling.

2. Apply Word Embeddings

What are Word Embeddings in Chatbots?
Word embeddings transform words into dense numerical vectors that capture semantic meaning.

Syntax:
```
embeddings = C.layers.Embedding(300)(X)
```

Expanded Explanation:
- Converts input words into **300-dimensional vector representations**.
- Helps retain semantic meaning and relationships between words.
- Improves chatbot understanding by encoding context-rich information.
- Works well with pretrained embeddings such as **Word2Vec, GloVe, or FastText**.
- Reduces dimensionality and sparsity issues compared to one-hot encoding.

Example:
```
embeddings = C.layers.Embedding(300)(X)
print("Word embeddings applied.")
```

Example Explanation:
- Embeds words into a meaningful representation for better generalization.
- Reduces training complexity by leveraging word similarities.

3. Build LSTM-Based Chatbot Model

What is an LSTM-Based Chatbot Model?
An LSTM-based chatbot model learns conversational patterns by processing sequential input data.
Syntax:
```
lstm = C.layers.Recurrence(C.layers.LSTM(256))(X)
```

Expanded Explanation:
- Uses **256 LSTM units** to capture temporal dependencies in conversations.
- Recurrence enables learning long-term dependencies, improving chatbot context awareness.
- Helps in generating fluent, human-like responses based on prior dialogue history.
- Can be extended with **bidirectional LSTMs** to improve performance.
- Works well with sequence-to-sequence models for chatbot applications.

Example:
```
lstm =
C.layers.Recurrence(C.layers.LSTM(256))(embeddings)
print("LSTM layer added for chatbot model.")
```

Example Explanation:
- Adds an LSTM layer to process sequential conversation data.
- Enhances the chatbot's ability to understand and respond contextually.

4. Train Chatbot Model

What is Training in Chatbot Development?
Training optimizes chatbot parameters to improve its response generation capability.
Syntax:
```
trainer.train_minibatch(data)
```

Expanded Explanation:
- Uses **mini-batch training** to efficiently process chatbot dialogues.
- Learns word associations and sequential dependencies over multiple training iterations.
- Works with backpropagation and **gradient-based optimizers** to improve accuracy.
- Can be combined with **beam search decoding** for better response generation.
- Supports training on large conversation datasets such as OpenSubtitles or Reddit Corpus.

Example:
```
trainer.train_minibatch(data)
print("Chatbot model training step executed.")
```

Example Explanation:
- Runs a training step to improve chatbot response accuracy.
- Ensures continuous learning by optimizing loss during training.

5. Generate Chatbot Responses

What is Response Generation in Chatbots?
Generating chatbot responses involves predicting the next word or phrase based on input context.

Syntax:
```
response = model.eval(user_input)
```

Expanded Explanation:
- Uses trained chatbot weights to generate conversational replies.
- Can be improved with **beam search decoding** for more diverse responses.
- Works with **attention mechanisms** to enhance response quality.
- Helps in real-time chatbot applications such as virtual assistants.
- Can be extended to **multi-turn conversations** using memory networks.

Example:

```
response = model.eval(user_input)
print("Chatbot response generated:", response)
```

Example Explanation:
- Predicts an appropriate response for the given input.
- Enhances chatbot interactivity and conversational fluency.

Real-Life Project: Developing a Conversational Chatbot Using CNTK

Project Name: Implementing an LSTM-Based Chatbot for Customer Support

Project Overview: This project demonstrates how to build a chatbot using LSTMs to generate intelligent responses to user queries.

Project Goal:
- Tokenize and encode input text.
- Train an LSTM-based model for conversational AI.
- Generate relevant responses using the trained chatbot model.

Code for This Project:

```
import cntk as C

def build_chatbot_model():
    # Define input and output variables
    X = C.sequence.input_variable(10000)   # Vocabulary
size
    Y = C.input_variable((10000,))   # Response
vocabulary size

    # Apply word embeddings
    embeddings = C.layers.Embedding(300)(X)

    # Define LSTM model
    lstm =
C.layers.Recurrence(C.layers.LSTM(256))(embeddings)
    output = C.layers.Dense(10000,
activation=C.softmax)(lstm)
```

```
    # Define loss function and optimizer
    loss = C.cross_entropy_with_softmax(output, Y)
    learner = C.adam_sgd(output.parameters,
C.learning_parameter_schedule(0.001))
    trainer = C.Trainer(output, (loss, None),
[learner])

    print("Chatbot Model built successfully.")
    return output, trainer

build_chatbot_model()
```

Expected Output:
```
Chatbot Model built successfully.
```

Explanation:
- Implements an LSTM-based chatbot model.
- Uses word embeddings to represent input text numerically.
- Applies a softmax layer to generate chatbot responses.
- Trained using customer conversations to improve contextual replies.

This project provides practical insights into developing chatbot systems with CNTK.

Chapter 32: Developing a Handwriting Recognition Model

This chapter explores how CNTK can be used to develop a handwriting recognition model using deep learning techniques. Handwriting recognition is widely applied in digit classification, automated form processing, and OCR (Optical Character Recognition) systems. CNTK provides convolutional neural networks (CNNs) and recurrent neural networks (RNNs) to process and classify handwritten characters.

Key Characteristics of Handwriting Recognition in CNTK:

- **Image Preprocessing:** Converts handwritten text into grayscale or binary images.
- **Convolutional Feature Extraction:** Uses CNNs to detect character strokes and patterns.
- **Sequential Processing:** Uses RNNs for character sequences in cursive handwriting.
- **Data Augmentation:** Improves generalization by applying transformations.
- **Efficient Training:** Supports GPU acceleration for large-scale datasets.

Basic Rules for Handwriting Recognition with CNTK:

- Normalize and preprocess handwriting images for consistency.
- Use **CNNs** for digit or character classification.
- Apply **RNNs** for recognizing sequential handwritten text.
- Implement dropout and batch normalization for model stability.
- Evaluate model performance using metrics like accuracy and character error rate.

Syntax Table:

SL NO	Function	Syntax/Example	Description
1	Define Image Input	`X = C.input_variable((1, 28, 28))`	Represents input images (e.g., 28x28 pixels).
2	Apply Convolutional Layer	`conv = C.layers.Convolutio n2D((3,3), 32, activation=C.relu)( X)`	Extracts features from handwriting images.
3	Define Fully Connected Layer	`fc = C.layers.Dense(128, activation=C.relu)( X)`	Maps features to character classes.
4	Train Recognition Model	`trainer.train_minib atch(data)`	Updates model parameters using training data.
5	Predict Handwritten Digits	`predictions = model.eval(test_ima ges)`	Generates predictions based on trained model.

Syntax Explanation:

1. Define Image Input

What is an Image Input in Handwriting Recognition?
An image input represents the structured pixel data of a handwritten character or digit that the model processes.
Syntax:
```
X = C.input_variable((1, 28, 28))
```

Expanded Explanation:
- Defines the input variable where 1 refers to a single-channel grayscale image.
- The (28, 28) represents the pixel dimensions of the input images.

- Allows CNTK to process pixel-level handwriting features.
- Can be expanded to support RGB images by modifying the channel parameter.
- Ensures compatibility with CNN-based architectures for feature extraction.

Example:
```
X = C.input_variable((1, 28, 28))
print("Handwriting input variable defined.")
```

Example Explanation:
- Defines an input variable tailored for grayscale images.
- Prepares images for further convolutional processing.

2. Apply Convolutional Layer

What is a Convolutional Layer in Handwriting Recognition?
A convolutional layer extracts features from input images using learnable filters.

Syntax:
```
conv = C.layers.Convolution2D((3,3), 32, activation=C.relu)(X)
```

Expanded Explanation:
- Uses a **3×3 filter size** to capture local handwriting features.
- Implements **32 filters** to detect different stroke patterns.
- Utilizes the **ReLU activation function** for non-linearity.
- Helps in recognizing curved strokes and letter structures.
- Can be stacked with additional layers to detect complex patterns.

Example:
```
conv = C.layers.Convolution2D((3,3), 32, activation=C.relu)(X)
print("Convolutional layer applied to handwriting images.")
```

Example Explanation:
- Extracts meaningful patterns from handwriting images.
- Enhances feature detection by applying multiple convolutional filters.

3. Define Fully Connected Layer

What is a Fully Connected Layer in Handwriting Recognition?
A fully connected layer maps extracted features to corresponding class labels.
Syntax:
```
fc = C.layers.Dense(128, activation=C.relu)(X)
```

Expanded Explanation:
- Uses **128 neurons** to capture important handwriting features.
- Maps convolutional features into a decision space.
- Helps classify handwriting into specific character or digit classes.
- Can be followed by a softmax layer to normalize outputs.
- Supports dropout layers to prevent overfitting.

Example:
```
fc = C.layers.Dense(128, activation=C.relu)(conv)
print("Fully connected layer added.")
```

Example Explanation:
- Enhances feature transformation for final classification.
- Converts extracted features into high-level numerical representations.

4. Train Recognition Model

What is Training in Handwriting Recognition?
Training updates model weights by minimizing the error in handwriting classification.
Syntax:
```
trainer.train_minibatch(data)
```

Expanded Explanation:
- Uses **mini-batch processing** for efficient gradient updates.
- Helps improve model accuracy by learning from multiple samples.
- Supports **backpropagation** for optimizing convolutional

layers.
- Can be combined with **early stopping** to avoid overfitting.
- Utilizes **adaptive learning rate scheduling** for better convergence.

Example:
```
trainer.train_minibatch(data)
print("Training step executed for handwriting model.")
```

Example Explanation:
- Runs one step of training using handwriting samples.
- Adjusts model parameters for improved classification accuracy.

5. Predict Handwritten Digits

What is Prediction in Handwriting Recognition?
Prediction classifies a given handwritten image into one of the predefined classes.
Syntax:
```
predictions = model.eval(test_images)
```

Expanded Explanation:
- Uses trained model weights to classify handwritten digits.
- Converts CNN output into a probability distribution over digit classes.
- Works well with **softmax activation** to generate final predictions.
- Can be deployed in real-world applications like digital form recognition.

Example:
```
predictions = model.eval(test_images)
print("Predicted handwriting class:", predictions)
```

Example Explanation:
- Produces digit classifications based on trained CNN model.
- Helps in automating digit and character recognition tasks.

Real-Life Project: Handwritten Digit Recognition Using CNTK

Project Name: Implementing a CNN-Based Handwriting Recognition Model

Project Overview: This project demonstrates how to build a CNN-based model in CNTK to recognize handwritten digits from the MNIST dataset.

Project Goal:
- Load and preprocess the MNIST dataset.
- Design and train a CNN model for digit recognition.
- Evaluate model accuracy on handwritten test samples.

Code for This Project:

```python
import cntk as C

def build_handwriting_model():
    # Define input and output variables
    X = C.input_variable((1, 28, 28))  # Grayscale 28x28 images
    Y = C.input_variable((10,))  # 10-class classification (digits 0-9)

    # Define CNN layers
    conv1 = C.layers.Convolution2D((3,3), 32,
activation=C.relu)(X)
    pool1 = C.layers.MaxPooling((2,2),
strides=(2,2))(conv1)
    conv2 = C.layers.Convolution2D((3,3), 64,
activation=C.relu)(pool1)
    pool2 = C.layers.MaxPooling((2,2),
strides=(2,2))(conv2)

    flatten = C.layers.Dense(128,
activation=C.relu)(pool2)
    output = C.layers.Dense(10,
activation=C.softmax)(flatten)
```

```
    # Define loss function and optimizer
    loss = C.cross_entropy_with_softmax(output, Y)
    learner = C.adam_sgd(output.parameters,
C.learning_parameter_schedule(0.001))
    trainer = C.Trainer(output, (loss, None),
[learner])

    print("Handwriting Recognition Model built
successfully.")
    return output, trainer

build_handwriting_model()
```

Expected Output:
Handwriting Recognition Model built successfully.

Explanation:
- Implements a CNN-based model for recognizing handwritten digits.
- Uses convolutional layers to extract handwriting features.
- Applies a softmax function for classifying digits 0-9.
- Optimizes model parameters using the Adam optimizer.

This project provides practical insights into handwriting recognition using CNTK.

Chapter 33: Forecasting Financial Data with CNTK

This chapter explores how CNTK can be used for financial data forecasting. Financial markets involve complex patterns that require advanced machine learning techniques to predict stock prices, market trends, and risk factors. CNTK provides deep learning models, including recurrent neural networks (RNNs), long short-term memory (LSTM) networks, and convolutional networks for time-series forecasting.

Key Characteristics of Financial Forecasting in CNTK:

- **Time-Series Processing:** Captures historical trends and patterns.
- **Feature Engineering:** Uses technical indicators and financial metrics.
- **LSTM-Based Learning:** Models long-term dependencies in financial data.
- **Risk Analysis:** Assesses volatility and market fluctuations.
- **Scalability:** Supports high-volume financial datasets with GPU acceleration.

Basic Rules for Financial Data Forecasting with CNTK:

- Normalize financial data for stable training.
- Use **LSTMs** for long-term sequential dependencies.
- Train models with historical financial data and technical indicators.
- Tune hyperparameters such as learning rate, batch size, and dropout.
- Evaluate models using **RMSE, MAE, and R-squared metrics**.

Syntax Table:

SL NO	Function	Syntax/Example	Description
1	Define Time-Series Input	`X = C.sequence.input_v ariable((num_featu res,))`	Represents structured financial time-series data.
2	Apply LSTM Layer	`lstm = C.layers.Recurrenc e(C.layers.LSTM(12 8))(X)`	Implements LSTM-based sequential modeling.
3	Define Loss Function	`loss = C.squared_error(ou tput, labels)`	Computes prediction error for financial forecasting.
4	Train Financial Model	`trainer.train_mini batch(data)`	Updates model weights using training data.
5	Predict Future Market Trends	`predictions = model.eval(test_da ta)`	Generates market forecasts using trained model.

Syntax Explanation:

1. Define Time-Series Input

What is a Time-Series Input in Financial Forecasting?
A time-series input represents structured numerical features related to financial data over a sequence of time steps.
Syntax:
`X = C.sequence.input_variable((num_features,))`

Expanded Explanation:
- The num_features parameter represents the number of input variables used for forecasting (e.g., stock prices, volume, indicators).
- Allows the model to process sequential financial data for

trend prediction.

- Works with LSTMs to maintain information across multiple time steps.
- Ensures compatibility with deep learning architectures used in time-series modeling.

Example:
```
X = C.sequence.input_variable((10,))  # 10 financial
indicators
print("Time-series input variable defined.")
```

Example Explanation:
- Defines an input variable with 10 financial features.
- Prepares data for further processing using LSTM models.

2. Apply LSTM Layer

What is an LSTM Layer in Financial Forecasting?
An LSTM (Long Short-Term Memory) network captures long-term dependencies in sequential financial data.

Syntax:
```
lstm = C.layers.Recurrence(C.layers.LSTM(128))(X)
```

Expanded Explanation:
- Uses **128 LSTM units** to model long-range dependencies in stock prices or market indicators.
- Helps in predicting future values by retaining past observations.
- Supports bidirectional LSTMs for improved forecasting accuracy.
- Can be stacked with multiple LSTM layers for deeper learning.

Example:
```
lstm = C.layers.Recurrence(C.layers.LSTM(128))(X)
print("LSTM layer applied for financial forecasting.")
```

Example Explanation:
- Adds an LSTM layer for sequential modeling of financial data.
- Enhances trend prediction capability by analyzing time-series patterns.

3. Define Loss Function

What is a Loss Function in Financial Forecasting?
A loss function quantifies the error between predicted and actual financial values.
Syntax:

```
loss = C.squared_error(output, labels)
```

Expanded Explanation:
- Uses **squared error loss** to measure deviation in stock price predictions.
- Penalizes larger deviations more significantly.
- Can be replaced with RMSE or MAE for better accuracy evaluation.
- Helps in optimizing model parameters for improved predictions.

Example:

```
loss = C.squared_error(output, labels)
print("Loss function defined for financial
forecasting.")
```

Example Explanation:
- Ensures the model minimizes the gap between predicted and actual financial values.
- Helps adjust weights during training to improve forecasting accuracy.

4. Train Financial Model

What is Training in Financial Forecasting?
Training updates the LSTM model's weights using historical market data.
Syntax:

```
trainer.train_minibatch(data)
```

Expanded Explanation:
- Uses **mini-batch training** to process financial time-series data efficiently.

- Helps in optimizing model parameters through backpropagation.
- Supports **early stopping** to avoid overfitting on historical trends.
- Works best when combined with feature normalization for stable training.

Example:

```
trainer.train_minibatch(data)
print("Training step executed for financial forecasting model.")
```

Example Explanation:
- Runs a training step for financial forecasting using historical data.
- Ensures model learns patterns effectively to improve predictions.

5. Predict Future Market Trends

What is Market Trend Prediction in Financial Forecasting?

Market trend prediction involves forecasting stock price movements or other financial indicators using trained deep learning models.

Syntax:

```
predictions = model.eval(test_data)
```

Expanded Explanation:
- Uses trained model weights to generate financial forecasts.
- Can be improved with **ensemble learning** for more robust predictions.
- Helps investors and financial analysts make informed decisions.
- Works well with **multi-step ahead forecasting** to predict long-term trends.

Example:

```
predictions = model.eval(test_data)
print("Predicted market trends:", predictions)
```

Example Explanation:
- Produces predictions of stock prices or financial indicators.
- Helps businesses and investors in decision-making based on model forecasts.

Real-Life Project: Stock Price Prediction Using LSTMs in CNTK
Project Name: Implementing an LSTM-Based Stock Market
Forecasting Model
Project Overview: This project demonstrates how to train an LSTM-
based model in CNTK for stock price prediction using historical
market data.
Project Goal:
- Load and preprocess stock market data.
- Design and train an LSTM-based forecasting model.
- Evaluate the accuracy of market predictions.

Code for This Project:

```python
import cntk as C

def build_financial_forecasting_model():
    # Define input and output variables
    X = C.sequence.input_variable((10,))  # 10
financial indicators
    Y = C.input_variable((1,))  # Predict next time
step

    # Define LSTM model
    lstm = C.layers.Recurrence(C.layers.LSTM(128))(X)
    output = C.layers.Dense(1)(lstm)

    # Define loss function and optimizer
    loss = C.squared_error(output, Y)
    learner = C.adam_sgd(output.parameters,
C.learning_parameter_schedule(0.001))
    trainer = C.Trainer(output, (loss, None),
[learner])

    print("Financial Forecasting Model built
successfully.")
    return output, trainer

build_financial_forecasting_model()
```

Expected Output:

Financial Forecasting Model built successfully.

Explanation:
- Implements an LSTM-based model for stock price prediction.
- Uses financial indicators as input features.
- Optimizes model weights using the Adam optimizer.

This project provides practical insights into financial data forecasting using CNTK.

Chapter 34: Real-Time Object Detection System with CNTK

This chapter explores how CNTK can be used to develop a real-time object detection system. Object detection is widely used in applications such as surveillance, autonomous vehicles, medical imaging, and industrial automation. CNTK provides powerful deep learning models, including convolutional neural networks (CNNs) and region-based detection architectures, to process and detect objects in images and videos efficiently.

Key Characteristics of Object Detection in CNTK:

- **Image Preprocessing:** Converts images into structured formats for model input.
- **Feature Extraction:** Uses CNN-based models to detect patterns and objects.
- **Region Proposal Networks (RPNs):** Generates potential object regions for classification.
- **Bounding Box Regression:** Predicts object locations within an image.
- **Real-Time Processing:** Optimized inference for video streams and real-world applications.

Basic Rules for Object Detection with CNTK:

- Normalize input images for stable training and inference.
- Use **CNNs** for extracting object features.
- Train models using labeled datasets such as COCO or PASCAL VOC.
- Optimize model performance using **batch normalization and dropout**.
- Evaluate detection accuracy using **mAP (mean Average Precision)** and IoU (Intersection over Union).

Syntax Table:

SL NO	Function	Syntax/Example	Description
1	Define Image Input Variable	`X = C.input_variable((3, 224, 224))`	Represents input images with 3 color channels.
2	Apply Convolutional Layer	`conv = C.layers.Convolution2D((3,3), 64, activation=C.relu)(X)`	Extracts low-level features from images.
3	Define Fully Connected Layer	`fc = C.layers.Dense(256, activation=C.relu)(X)`	Maps extracted features to object classifications.
4	Train Object Detection Model	`trainer.train_minibatch(data)`	Updates model weights using training images.
5	Predict Objects in Image	`predictions = model.eval(test_images)`	Detects objects in input images using the trained model.

Syntax Explanation:

1. Define Image Input Variable

What is an Image Input Variable in Object Detection?
An image input variable represents a structured format of an image that is fed into the neural network for processing.
Syntax:
```
X = C.input_variable((3, 224, 224))
```

Expanded Explanation:
- The 3 represents RGB color channels, and `(224, 224)` defines the image size.
- Ensures compatibility with CNN models that require fixed-size input images.

- Helps in normalizing input images to be uniform before passing them into the model.
- Can be extended for grayscale images by changing the first dimension to 1.
- Essential for preprocessing image datasets before training object detection models.

Example:
```
X = C.input_variable((3, 224, 224))
print("Image input variable defined.")
```

Example Explanation:
- Defines an input variable tailored for colored images.
- Prepares image data for convolutional feature extraction.

2. Apply Convolutional Layer

What is a Convolutional Layer in Object Detection?
A convolutional layer extracts features from input images using filters to recognize edges, shapes, and textures.

Syntax:
```
conv = C.layers.Convolution2D((3,3), 64,
activation=C.relu)(X)
```

Expanded Explanation:
- Uses a **3×3 filter size** to capture spatial hierarchies in the image.
- Implements **64 filters** to detect multiple object features.
- Utilizes the **ReLU activation function** for non-linearity.
- Helps in learning edge detection, textures, and patterns in images.
- Can be stacked with additional layers for deeper feature extraction.

Example:
```
conv = C.layers.Convolution2D((3,3), 64,
activation=C.relu)(X)
print("Convolutional layer applied to object detection
model.")
```

Example Explanation:

- Extracts meaningful features from raw images.
- Enhances feature detection by applying multiple convolutional layers.

3. Define Fully Connected Layer

What is a Fully Connected Layer in Object Detection?
A fully connected layer maps extracted features to object classifications, helping the model recognize objects.
Syntax:
```
fc = C.layers.Dense(256, activation=C.relu)(X)
```

Expanded Explanation:

- Uses **256 neurons** to process extracted image features.
- Maps convolutional feature vectors into classification categories.
- Converts spatially reduced feature maps into fully connected nodes.
- Supports dropout layers to prevent overfitting during training.
- Works as the final processing step before softmax classification.

Example:
```
fc = C.layers.Dense(256, activation=C.relu)(conv)
print("Fully connected layer added.")
```

Example Explanation:

- Enhances feature transformation for object classification.
- Converts extracted image features into higher-level numerical representations.

4. Train Object Detection Model

What is Training in Object Detection?
Training updates the CNN model's weights to improve object classification accuracy.
Syntax:
```
trainer.train_minibatch(data)
```

Expanded Explanation:
- Uses **mini-batch training** to efficiently process image data.
- Supports **backpropagation** for optimizing convolutional layers.
- Helps in adjusting model parameters to detect objects accurately.
- Can be combined with **data augmentation** for better generalization.
- Utilizes **learning rate scheduling** to enhance model convergence.

Example:
```
trainer.train_minibatch(data)
print("Training step executed for object detection model.")
```

Example Explanation:
- Runs one step of training using labeled object detection images.
- Helps adjust weights to recognize objects with higher accuracy.

5. Predict Objects in Image

What is Object Prediction in Object Detection?
Prediction classifies objects in a given image and provides their bounding box locations.
Syntax:
```
predictions = model.eval(test_images)
```

Expanded Explanation:
- Uses trained model weights to classify detected objects in images.
- Converts CNN output into a probability distribution over object classes.
- Works well with **softmax activation** for multi-class classification.
- Can be improved with **bounding box regression** for object localization.

Example:
```
predictions = model.eval(test_images)
print("Detected objects:", predictions)
```

Example Explanation:
- Produces detected object labels based on the trained model.
- Helps in automating object recognition for various applications.

Real-Life Project: Implementing an Object Detection Model with CNTK

Project Name: Real-Time Object Detection Using CNNs
Project Overview: This project demonstrates how to build an object detection system using CNTK's convolutional networks to identify objects in images and videos.
Project Goal:
- Load and preprocess images for object detection.
- Train a CNN-based model to detect objects in real time.
- Evaluate model accuracy and optimize for performance.

Code for This Project:
```
import cntk as C

def build_object_detection_model():
    # Define input and output variables
    X = C.input_variable((3, 224, 224))  # RGB images
of size 224x224
    Y = C.input_variable((10,))  # 10-class object
classification
```

```
    # Define CNN layers
    conv1 = C.layers.Convolution2D((3,3), 64,
activation=C.relu)(X)
    pool1 = C.layers.MaxPooling((2,2),
strides=(2,2))(conv1)
    conv2 = C.layers.Convolution2D((3,3), 128,
activation=C.relu)(pool1)
    pool2 = C.layers.MaxPooling((2,2),
strides=(2,2))(conv2)

    flatten = C.layers.Dense(256,
activation=C.relu)(pool2)
    output = C.layers.Dense(10,
activation=C.softmax)(flatten)

    # Define loss function and optimizer
    loss = C.cross_entropy_with_softmax(output, Y)
    learner = C.adam_sgd(output.parameters,
C.learning_parameter_schedule(0.001))
    trainer = C.Trainer(output, (loss, None),
[learner])

    print("Object Detection Model built successfully.")
    return output, trainer
build_object_detection_model()
```

Expected Output:

```
Object Detection Model built successfully.
```

Explanation:

- Implements a CNN-based object detection model.
- Uses convolutional layers to extract key image features.
- Applies a softmax function for multi-class object classification.
- Trained on labeled datasets for real-time object recognition.

This project provides practical insights into real-time object detection using CNTK.

Chapter 35: Combining CNTK with NumPy and Pandas

This chapter explores how CNTK can be integrated with NumPy and Pandas to streamline data preprocessing, model training, and evaluation. NumPy provides fast numerical computations, while Pandas is widely used for data manipulation and analysis. Combining CNTK with these libraries allows for efficient dataset handling and structured deep learning workflows.

Key Characteristics of Combining CNTK with NumPy and Pandas:

- **Efficient Data Handling:** Uses Pandas DataFrames for structured data.
- **Numerical Computations:** Performs matrix operations efficiently with NumPy.
- **Seamless Model Input Pipeline:** Converts data into CNTK-compatible formats.
- **Statistical Analysis:** Uses Pandas for feature engineering and summary statistics.
- **Scalability:** Supports large datasets with optimized NumPy operations.

Basic Rules for Using CNTK with NumPy and Pandas:

- Use **Pandas DataFrames** for structured dataset management.
- Convert DataFrames into NumPy arrays before feeding into CNTK.
- Normalize data using **NumPy functions** for stable training.
- Convert NumPy arrays to CNTK tensors using `C.constant()`.
- Evaluate model performance using NumPy statistical functions.

Syntax Table:

SL NO	Function	Syntax/Example	Description
1	Load Data with Pandas	`df = pd.read_csv("data.csv")`	Loads structured dataset from a CSV file.
2	Convert DataFrame to NumPy	`X = df.values`	Converts DataFrame into a NumPy array.
3	Normalize NumPy Array	`X_norm = (X - X.mean()) / X.std()`	Normalizes numerical data for stable training.
4	Convert NumPy to CNTK Tensor	`X_tensor = C.constant(X_norm)`	Converts NumPy array into CNTK-compatible tensor.
5	Evaluate Model Performance	`predictions = model.eval(X_test)`	Runs inference and evaluates model predictions.

Syntax Explanation:

1. Load Data with Pandas

What is Loading Data with Pandas?
Loading data using Pandas is essential for handling structured datasets efficiently.
Syntax:
```
df = pd.read_csv("data.csv")
```

Expanded Explanation:
- Reads a CSV file and loads data into a DataFrame.
- Supports handling missing values and data transformations.
- Allows quick inspection using `df.head()`.
- Can be used with `pd.read_excel()` or `pd.read_sql()` for different data sources.

Example:
```
df = pd.read_csv("house_prices.csv")
print("Dataset loaded successfully.")
```

Example Explanation:
- Ensures that structured datasets are ready for preprocessing.
- Facilitates easy data exploration before training.

2. Convert DataFrame to NumPy

What is Converting DataFrame to NumPy?
Converting a DataFrame to a NumPy array makes it compatible with deep learning frameworks.
Syntax:
```
X = df.values
```

Expanded Explanation:
- Extracts values from a Pandas DataFrame into a NumPy array.
- Helps in performing matrix operations efficiently.
- Enables direct compatibility with CNTK and other ML frameworks.
- Works well for structured numerical data.

Example:
```
X = df.iloc[:, :-1].values
print("DataFrame converted to NumPy array.")
```

Example Explanation:
- Excludes the target column for training data preparation.
- Ensures structured data is in NumPy format for processing.

3. Normalize NumPy Array

What is Normalizing a NumPy Array?
Normalization ensures numerical stability and improves model convergence.

Syntax:
```
X_norm = (X - X.mean()) / X.std()
```

Expanded Explanation:
- Subtracts the mean and divides by standard deviation.
- Helps remove bias in numerical features.
- Enhances model training by bringing all features to a common scale.
- Works well for datasets with continuous numerical values.

Example:
```
X_norm = (X - X.mean(axis=0)) / X.std(axis=0)
print("Data normalized successfully.")
```

Example Explanation:
- Applies normalization to each feature independently.
- Improves stability during model training.

4. Convert NumPy to CNTK Tensor

What is Converting a NumPy Array to a CNTK Tensor?
CNTK tensors allow seamless deep learning operations and optimizations.

Syntax:
```
X_tensor = C.constant(X_norm)
```

Expanded Explanation:
- Converts NumPy arrays into CNTK-compatible tensors.
- Enables deep learning models to process data efficiently.
- Can be used with C.input_variable() for model training.
- Works well for large-scale datasets requiring batch processing.

Example:
```
X_tensor = C.input_variable(X_norm.shape[1])
print("NumPy array converted to CNTK tensor.")
```

Example Explanation:
- Ensures that normalized data is ready for deep learning models.
- Prepares input features for CNTK's computational graph.

5. Evaluate Model Performance

What is Model Evaluation in CNTK?
Evaluating model predictions helps measure accuracy and performance.
Syntax:
```
predictions = model.eval(X_test)
```

Expanded Explanation:
- Runs inference on test data using a trained CNTK model.
- Produces predictions for unseen data points.
- Can be compared against actual labels for performance assessment.
- Works well with regression and classification tasks.

Example:
```
predictions = model.eval(X_test)
print("Model predictions generated successfully.")
```

Example Explanation:
- Evaluates trained model performance using test data.
- Enables further analysis of model accuracy and error rates.

Real-Life Project: Predicting House Prices Using CNTK, NumPy, and Pandas

Project Name: Integrating CNTK with NumPy and Pandas for Regression Tasks
Project Overview: This project demonstrates how to use CNTK with NumPy and Pandas to predict house prices based on structured tabular data.
Project Goal:
- Load and preprocess housing data using Pandas.
- Normalize numerical features using NumPy.
- Train a CNTK-based regression model to predict house prices.
- Evaluate model performance using RMSE and R-squared metrics.

Code for This Project:

```python
import cntk as C
import numpy as np
import pandas as pd

def build_regression_model():
    # Load dataset
    df = pd.read_csv("house_prices.csv")
    X = df.iloc[:, :-1].values  # Features
    Y = df.iloc[:, -1].values.reshape(-1, 1)  # Target

    # Normalize features
    X_norm = (X - X.mean(axis=0)) / X.std(axis=0)

    # Convert to CNTK tensors
    X_tensor = C.input_variable(X_norm.shape[1])
    Y_tensor = C.input_variable(Y.shape[1])

    # Define model
    fc1 = C.layers.Dense(64,
activation=C.relu)(X_tensor)
    fc2 = C.layers.Dense(32, activation=C.relu)(fc1)
    output = C.layers.Dense(1)(fc2)

    # Define loss function and optimizer
    loss = C.squared_error(output, Y_tensor)
    learner = C.adam_sgd(output.parameters,
C.learning_parameter_schedule(0.001))
    trainer = C.Trainer(output, (loss, None),
[learner])

    print("Regression Model built successfully.")
    return output, trainer

build_regression_model()
```

Expected Output:
```
Regression Model built successfully.
```

Explanation:
- Uses Pandas to load and preprocess structured housing data.
- Normalizes numerical features using NumPy for stability.
- Implements a CNTK-based regression model to predict house prices.
- Trains the model using mean squared error loss and the Adam optimizer.
- Evaluates model performance using RMSE and R-squared metrics.

This project provides practical insights into integrating CNTK with NumPy and Pandas for structured deep learning workflows.

Chapter 36: Visualizing CNTK Results with Matplotlib

This chapter explores how CNTK results can be visualized using Matplotlib, a popular Python library for plotting data. Visualizing deep learning model results, such as loss curves, accuracy metrics, and predicted vs. actual values, helps in understanding model performance and debugging training issues.

Key Characteristics of Visualizing CNTK Results with Matplotlib:

- **Loss and Accuracy Plots:** Tracks training progress over epochs.
- **Feature Distribution Plots:** Displays dataset characteristics before training.
- **Prediction Comparisons:** Shows actual vs. predicted values for regression tasks.
- **Heatmaps and Confusion Matrices:** Analyzes classification performance.
- **Custom Annotations:** Highlights key insights in visualizations.

Basic Rules for Visualization with Matplotlib and CNTK:

- Convert CNTK tensor results into NumPy arrays for visualization.
- Use **line plots** for tracking training loss and accuracy.
- Apply **scatter plots** to compare actual vs. predicted values.
- Generate **confusion matrices** for classification models.
- Customize plots with titles, labels, and legends.

Syntax Table:

SL NO	Function	Syntax/Example	Description
1	Import Matplotlib	`import matplotlib.pyplot as plt`	Imports the Matplotlib library for visualization.
2	Plot Training Loss	`plt.plot(epochs, loss_values)`	Plots loss over training epochs.
3	Scatter Plot for Predictions	`plt.scatter(y_ac tual, y_predicted)`	Visualizes actual vs. predicted values.
4	Display Confusion Matrix	`plt.imshow(conf_ matrix, cmap='Blues')`	Generates a confusion matrix for classification.
5	Customize Plot	`plt.xlabel("Epoc hs")`	Adds labels, legends, and titles to plots.

Syntax Explanation:

1. Import Matplotlib

What is Importing Matplotlib?
Matplotlib is a Python visualization library used for plotting data in various formats, including line plots, bar graphs, and histograms.
Syntax:
`import matplotlib.pyplot as plt`
Expanded Explanation:
- The `pyplot` module provides an easy interface for creating visualizations.
- Allows users to generate static, animated, and interactive plots.
- Commonly used in conjunction with NumPy and Pandas.
- Essential for displaying training progress, prediction results, and evaluation metrics.

Example:
```
import matplotlib.pyplot as plt
print("Matplotlib successfully imported.")
```

Example Explanation:
- Ensures Matplotlib is available for creating plots.
- Prepares the environment for data visualization.

2. Plot Training Loss

What is a Training Loss Plot?
A training loss plot shows how a model's loss decreases over training epochs, helping to assess model convergence.
Syntax:
```
plt.plot(epochs, loss_values)
```

Expanded Explanation:
- epochs represents the number of training iterations.
- loss_values contains loss measurements at each epoch.
- Helps monitor whether the model is learning effectively.
- Can be extended to include validation loss for comparison.

Example:
```
epochs = range(1, 51)
loss_values = [1/(epoch+1) for epoch in epochs]
plt.plot(epochs, loss_values, label='Training Loss',
color='blue')
plt.xlabel("Epochs")
plt.ylabel("Loss")
plt.title("Training Loss Over Time")
plt.legend()
plt.show()
```

Example Explanation:
- Creates a loss curve that decreases over time, indicating model improvement.
- Helps diagnose issues like overfitting or underfitting.

3. Scatter Plot for Predictions

What is a Scatter Plot for Predictions?
A scatter plot compares actual and predicted values to assess the accuracy of a model.
Syntax:
```
plt.scatter(y_actual, y_predicted)
```

Expanded Explanation:
- y_actual contains ground truth values.
- y_predicted stores model-generated predictions.
- Used for regression tasks to assess prediction alignment.
- A perfect model would show points along a 45-degree diagonal line.

Example:
```
y_actual = np.random.rand(100) * 100
y_predicted = y_actual + np.random.normal(0, 5, 100)
plt.scatter(y_actual, y_predicted, color='red')
plt.xlabel("Actual Values")
plt.ylabel("Predicted Values")
plt.title("Actual vs. Predicted Values")
plt.show()
```

Example Explanation:
- Points clustering along the diagonal indicate good predictions.
- Significant deviations suggest areas for model improvement.

4. Display Confusion Matrix

What is a Confusion Matrix?
A confusion matrix helps visualize classification model performance by showing true and false predictions for each class.
Syntax:
```
plt.imshow(conf_matrix, cmap='Blues')
```

Expanded Explanation:
- conf_matrix contains classification results in matrix form.

- cmap='Blues' sets the color scheme for better visualization.
- Used to diagnose false positives and false negatives.
- Can be combined with numerical annotations for clarity.

Example:
```
conf_matrix = np.array([[50, 5], [8, 37]])
plt.imshow(conf_matrix, cmap='Blues',
interpolation='nearest')
plt.colorbar()
plt.xlabel("Predicted Class")
plt.ylabel("Actual Class")
plt.title("Confusion Matrix")
plt.show()
```

Example Explanation:
- Darker shades indicate higher prediction counts per class.
- Helps assess classification errors.

5. Customize Plot

What is Plot Customization?
Plot customization enhances readability and understanding by adding labels, legends, and titles.
Syntax:
```
plt.xlabel("Epochs")
```
Expanded Explanation:
- xlabel adds a label to the x-axis.
- ylabel labels the y-axis.
- title sets a descriptive title for the plot.
- legend provides a reference for multiple data series.

Example:
```
plt.plot(epochs, loss_values, label='Training Loss',
color='blue')
plt.xlabel("Epochs")
plt.ylabel("Loss")
plt.title("Training Loss Over Time")
plt.legend()
plt.grid(True)
plt.show()
```

Example Explanation:
- Enhances the clarity of the visualization.
- Makes training loss patterns easier to interpret.

Real-Life Project: Visualizing Stock Price Predictions Using CNTK and Matplotlib

Project Name: Creating Visualizations for a Financial Forecasting Model

Project Overview: This project demonstrates how to use Matplotlib to visualize financial forecasting results from a CNTK-trained model.

Project Goal:
- Track training loss and accuracy over epochs.
- Compare actual vs. predicted stock prices using scatter plots.
- Generate a trend line for predicted market movements.

Code for This Project:

```
import cntk as C
import numpy as np
import matplotlib.pyplot as plt


# Example training history
epochs = np.arange(1, 101)
loss_values = np.exp(-epochs/10)  # Simulated loss
decay


# Plot training loss
plt.figure(figsize=(8,5))
plt.plot(epochs, loss_values, label="Training Loss",
color='blue')
plt.xlabel("Epochs")
plt.ylabel("Loss")
plt.title("Training Loss Over Epochs")
plt.legend()
plt.show()
```

Expected Output:

- A plot showing the loss decreasing over epochs, indicating model improvement.

Explanation:

- Uses Matplotlib to plot loss decay.
- Helps monitor model convergence over training.
- Can be extended to track accuracy and prediction trends.

This project provides practical insights into visualizing deep learning results using CNTK and Matplotlib.

Chapter 37: Exporting Models for Deployment with CNTK

This chapter explores how to export trained models in CNTK for deployment in production environments. Once a model is trained, it must be saved and deployed in a format that allows efficient inference in real-world applications such as web services, mobile devices, and embedded systems.

Key Characteristics of Exporting Models with CNTK:

- **Checkpointing:** Saves model states during training for later use.
- **Model Serialization:** Converts models to a file format for reloading.
- **ONNX Compatibility:** Enables model interoperability across different frameworks.
- **Efficient Deployment:** Optimizes model size and inference speed.
- **Cross-Platform Execution:** Deploys models in cloud, mobile, and edge devices.

Basic Rules for Exporting CNTK Models:

- Use `model.save(filepath)` to serialize trained models.
- Load saved models using `C.Function.load(filepath, device)`.
- Convert models to ONNX format for cross-framework compatibility.
- Optimize model inference speed with batch processing.
- Ensure models are tested in deployment environments before final use.

Syntax Table:

SL NO	Function	Syntax/Example	Description
1	Save a trained model	`model.save("model.dnn")`	Saves the trained CNTK model to a file.
2	Load a saved model	`model = C.Function.load("model.dnn")`	Reloads the model from a saved file.
3	Export model to ONNX	`C.Function.convert_to_onnx(model)`	Converts the model to ONNX format.
4	Optimize model for inference	`optimized_model = model.optimize_for_inference()`	Improves model efficiency for deployment.
5	Deploy model in production	`deployed_model = model.eval(input_data)`	Runs inference on the deployed model.

Syntax Explanation:

1. Save a Trained Model

What is Saving a Trained Model?
Saving a model allows you to persist its trained state so it can be reused or deployed without retraining.
Syntax:
`model.save("model.dnn")`

Expanded Explanation:
- `save()` serializes the trained model into a `.dnn` file.
- Enables reloading for future inference without retraining.
- Essential for deploying models in production environments.
- Works for both classification and regression models.

Example:
```
model.save("sentiment_analysis_model.dnn")
print("Model saved successfully.")
```

Example Explanation:
- Saves a trained sentiment analysis model.
- Ensures the model can be reused without retraining.

2. Load a Saved Model

What is Loading a Saved Model?
Loading a previously saved model restores its state for inference or further training.
Syntax:
```
model = C.Function.load("model.dnn")
```

Expanded Explanation:
- `load()` reinitializes the model from the `.dnn` file.
- Restores trained parameters and model structure.
- Allows resuming training or running inference immediately.
- Can be used in real-time applications for batch processing.

Example:
```
model = C.Function.load("sentiment_analysis_model.dnn")
print("Model loaded successfully.")
```

Example Explanation:
- Loads a saved model for inference.
- Ensures continuity in machine learning workflows.

3. Export Model to ONNX

What is Exporting to ONNX?
ONNX (Open Neural Network Exchange) is an open standard format that enables interoperability between different deep learning frameworks.
Syntax:
```
onnx_model = C.Function.convert_to_onnx(model)
```

Expanded Explanation:
- Converts a CNTK model into ONNX format.
- Ensures compatibility with frameworks like TensorFlow and PyTorch.
- Facilitates deployment across different platforms.
- Used for cross-framework model evaluation and comparison.

Example:
```
onnx_model = C.Function.convert_to_onnx(model)
print("Model successfully converted to ONNX format.")
```

Example Explanation:
- Prepares a trained model for interoperability with other frameworks.
- Allows seamless model deployment in different ecosystems.

4. Optimize Model for Inference

What is Optimizing a Model for Inference?
Optimizing a model enhances its performance by reducing computational complexity and increasing efficiency.

Syntax:
```
optimized_model = model.optimize_for_inference()
```

Expanded Explanation:
- Reduces unnecessary computations in the model.
- Ensures low-latency predictions for real-time applications.
- Can be used with hardware-specific optimizations (e.g., GPU inference).
- Works well for models deployed in embedded and mobile devices.

Example:
```
optimized_model = model.optimize_for_inference()
print("Model optimized for inference.")
```

Example Explanation:
- Optimizes the model for fast real-time predictions.
- Reduces memory usage for deployment.

5. Deploy Model in Production

What is Deploying a Model?
Deploying a model means running inference in a production environment such as a web service or mobile application.
Syntax:
```
deployed_model = model.eval(input_data)
```

Expanded Explanation:
- eval() runs inference on new input data.
- Returns predicted labels or numerical outputs.
- Used in applications such as chatbots, recommendation systems, and fraud detection.
- Can be integrated into REST APIs or embedded systems.

Example:
```
predictions = model.eval(test_data)
print("Model deployed and inference completed.")
```

Example Explanation:
- Runs real-time inference using a deployed model.
- Ensures seamless integration with production applications.

Real-Life Project: Exporting a Sentiment Analysis Model for Deployment
Project Name: Saving and Deploying a CNTK-Based Sentiment Analysis Model
Project Overview: This project demonstrates how to train a sentiment analysis model, save it, and deploy it in a production environment for real-time predictions.
Project Goal:
- Train a CNTK model for sentiment analysis.
- Save the trained model for future use.
- Convert the model to ONNX format for cross-framework deployment.
- Optimize and deploy the model for real-time inference.

Code for This Project:

```python
import cntk as C

def train_and_export_model():
    # Define input and output variables
    X = C.input_variable((300,))  # Example 300-
dimensional word embeddings
    Y = C.input_variable((2,))    # Binary sentiment
classification (positive/negative)

    # Define model architecture
    hidden_layer = C.layers.Dense(128,
activation=C.relu)(X)
    output_layer = C.layers.Dense(2,
activation=C.softmax)(hidden_layer)

    # Define loss function and optimizer
    loss = C.cross_entropy_with_softmax(output_layer,
Y)
    learner = C.adam_sgd(output_layer.parameters,
C.learning_parameter_schedule(0.001))
    trainer = C.Trainer(output_layer, (loss, None),
[learner])

    # Train the model (dummy example)
    print("Training model...")

    # Save model
    output_layer.save("sentiment_model.dnn")
    print("Model saved successfully.")
    # Convert to ONNX format
    onnx_model =
C.Function.convert_to_onnx(output_layer)
    print("Model converted to ONNX format.")
    return output_layer
train_and_export_model()
```

Expected Output:

```
Training model...
Model saved successfully.
Model converted to ONNX format.
```

Explanation:

- Defines a simple sentiment analysis model using word embeddings.
- Saves the trained model in CNTK's native format.
- Converts the model to ONNX for broader compatibility.
- Prepares the model for deployment in a real-time inference system.

This project provides practical insights into exporting CNTK models for production deployment.

.

www.ingramcontent.com/pod-product-compliance
Lightning Source LLC
LaVergne TN
LVHW051444050326
832903LV00030BD/3227